Welcome to the Peace of Mind® Community!

Stay Informed
Peace of Mind's monthly newsletter includes practices you can use in the classroom and information about events, training, and resources. Join the mailing list on our website.

Get Support
If you are new to Peace of Mind, you will find our short online course "Getting Started with Peace of Mind" helpful. Visit the **Educators** page on our website.

Prepare to Teach
You can find links to the materials you need for this curriculum on our website under **Shop**.

TeachPeaceofMind.org

Questions? Comments?
We'd love to hear from you!
info@TeachPeaceofMind.org

- peaceofminddc
- @TeachPeaceofMind
- @peaceofmindorg

Peace of Mind Core Curriculum for Early Childhood

Peace of Mind Core Curriculum for First and Second Grade

Peace of Mind Core Curriculum for Third Grade

Peace of Mind Curriculum for Fourth and Fifth Grade

Peace of Mind Core Curriculum for Middle School

Peace of Mind Social Justice Lesson Supplement for Grades 3-5

Henry and Friends Storybooks

Classroom Resources, Training, Community of Practice

TeachPeaceofMind.org

Peace of Mind Inc, Washington, D.C. 20015
Https://TeachPeaceofMind.org
Copyright 2021 Peace of Mind Inc.

Peace of Mind® is a registered trademark of Peace of Mind Inc. All rights reserved. No part of this curriculum may be reproduced, stored in a retrieval system, or transmitted by any means, electronic or otherwise, without prior written permission from the author. Please contact Peace of Mind Inc. via TeachPeaceofMind.org to request permission.

Cover and Interior Design: Schwa Design Group
Illustrations: Gigi Gonyea and Linda Ryden
Photo Credits: Linda Ryden
Logo: Pittny Creative

ISBN 978-1-7373423-2-8
Library of Congress Control Number: 2021918758
Published 2021

Praise for The *Peace of Mind* Curriculum Series

I am astounded by this beautiful curriculum. Linda and her colleagues have created a brilliantly practical guide for teachers, one that understands kids — both how they think, and their imaginative capacities.... This is a model for the classroom of the future.

Jeff Warren, Author and Meditation Teacher

You have done such an outstanding job and this is such a comprehensive curriculum. I am implementing your program...and strongly encouraging my colleagues in our district to do so also.

Cathy Stainbrook, M.A.E, Professional School Counselor

I started using the curriculum and it's wonderful! The lessons are easy to follow and very well thought out. The curriculum fits well with the Mindful Schools training that I did a few years ago. I'm very pleased with my purchase.

Kree Barus, Grade 2 Learning Support Teacher

This is an extraordinary curriculum, at once practical and visionary. The lessons are thoughtfully and meticulously scaffolded as the children are guided step-by-step into an understanding of how their brains work, how to interact with the world with kindness, and how to master themselves. In this age of anxiety, what could be more important or valuable than to teach children at an early age how to interpret and navigate their big emotions, calm themselves, and by extension, each other?

Val Carroll, Early Childhood Arts Integration Educator

We want our children to master their academics but we equally want them to master being good citizens who care about one another and the world at large. The Peace [of Mind] Program does just that. In an age where bullying has become a major problem, the Program is proactive instead of reactive, thereby eliminating some of those problems before they begin.

Jackie Snowden, former Assistant Principal

The importance of teaching kindness, compassion, how to get along, what to do if there is bullying, and how to handle or possibly to avoid conflicts cannot be overstated. The Peace [of Mind] program works. We have been able to see the difference between the students' ability to handle conflicts over the years and we have seen improvement.

Lisa Jensen and Blake Yedwab, Elementary School Teachers

Praise for the *Henry and Friends* Storybook Series

These delightful, captivating books are full of powerful practical methods for kids — and their parents.

                          Rick Hanson, Ph.D., author of *Resilient, Hardwiring Happiness,* and *Buddha's Brain*

Marleigh is Mindful is a brilliant book of simple and creative mindfulness interventions by an educator who gets children….By framing practice as fundamentally playful, this book brings the benefits of mindfulness and compassion to a new generation. An indispensable toolkit for every classroom and home.

                          Jeff Warren, Author and Meditation Teacher

In this simple and clear story, Tyaja Uses the Think Test, *Linda Ryden offers valuable lessons for our children to bring more clarity, care, and thoughtfulness to the power of words.*

                          Oren Jay Sofer, author of *Say What You Mean: A Mindful Approach to Nonviolent Communication*

Linda Ryden's kids' book about Heartfulness practice, Henry is Kind, *is bright, fun, and engaging, which is wonderful because it means kids will love it. And the book provides an easy way for teachers and parents to help children understand and enjoy being kind, which means adults will love it too. It is a pleasure to think of the benefits* Henry is Kind *may bring to children and families.*

                          Sharon Salzberg, author of *Real Happiness and Real Love*

I absolutely adore Sergio Sees the Good. *It's a really relatable story for both kids and adults. The science is just right — totally accessible but not "dumbed down." I love the part about the cactus because you show that it's not all bad to focus on the negative stuff and there's a logical reason why evolution didn't do away with it. I think it's also great that you touched on how one can overcome the negativity bias in daily life by noticing and feeling grateful for the "little, good things," even though that feels more effortful.*

                          Dr. Elizabeth Hoffman, Neuroscientist

Contents

Introduction — 1
Curriculum Overview — 3
Preparing to Teach — 8
Peace of Mind for Third Graders — 13
Curriculum At-a-Glance — 15

Unit 1: Mindfulness Foundations
- Week 1: Introduction to Mindfulness — 22
- Week 2: Mindful Listening, Mindful Seeing — 28
- Week 3: Four Square Breathing — 34
- Week 4: Create Your Own Breath — 39
- Week 5: Peaceful Place Visualization — 43

Unit 2: Gratitude and the Negativity Bias
- Week 6: Sergio Sees the Good — 48
- Week 7: Gratitude Marble Game — 52
- Week 8: Little Good Things — 56

Unit 3: Metacognition
- Week 9: Mindfulness of Thoughts — 62
- Week 10: Thought Catcher — 66
- Week 11: Time Traveling — 70
- Week 12: Keeping Your Focus — 75

Unit 4: Feelings, Sensations, and Your Body
- Week 13: Using Mindfulness to Take Care of Anger — 82
- Week 14: Body Scan — 88
- Week 15: Tummy Breaths — 93
- Week 16: Squeeze and Release — 98
- Week 17: Mindful Eating — 102

Unit 5: Kindness and Compassion
- Week 18: Kindness Chain — 108
- Week 19: Heartfulness — 112
- Week 20: Empathy — 116

Unit 6: Brain Science
- Week 21: Rosie's Brain — 122
- Week 22: Helping Amy: Amygdala — 125
- Week 23: Who's the Boss? Prefrontal Cortex — 132
- Week 24: Do You Remember? Hippocampus — 138

Unit 7: Applied Mindfulness: Conflict Resolution

- Week 25: Learn about Conflict with Zion and Zuri — 144
- Week 26: The Conflict Escalator — 149
- Week 27: Conflict Escalator Practice: The Class Party — 154
- Week 28: MOFL or Awful? — 159
- Week 29: The Conflict C.A.T. — 164
- Week 30: More about the Conflict Toolbox — 168
- Week 31: Conflict C.A.T. Role Play 1 — 174
- Week 32: Conflict C.A.T. Role Play 2 — 178

End-of-Year Activity

- Week 33: Kindest Things — 184

Resources — 189

- Program Extensions — 190
- Reproducible Materials — 192
- Teacher Resources — 214

Bibliography — 216

Credits — 217

Appreciation and Acknowledgements — 218

Author and Illustrator Bios — 220

Introduction

Supporting students' social and emotional well-being has never been more important. As we write this our kids and educators are coping with anxiety and fear related to the Covid-19 pandemic and facing great uncertainty about returning to school. Before 2020 we knew that we had some students who had experienced some sort of trauma; we know now that all of our students have been through a deeply traumatic experience.

Since we published our first *Peace of Mind Curriculum* in 2016, we have continued to learn and develop the Peace of Mind Program with Linda's students in the dynamic setting of a public school classroom here in Washington D.C. We have also had the good fortune to receive feedback and stories from educators using the *Peace of Mind Curriculum* in a wide variety of educational settings.

One thing we learned is that we needed to divide our very first publication, the *Peace of Mind Core Curriculum for Grades 3-5,* into two separate volumes. We published the *Peace of Mind Curriculum for Grades 4 & 5* in 2019. We are thrilled to now share this new guide with you: a revised set of lessons just for third grade. Even if you have been using the *Core Curriculum for Grades 3-5*, you will find new lessons and approaches here.

To help you meet the needs of all of your third graders, we have incorporated trauma-informed practices throughout this curriculum. You will notice a larger focus on understanding and practicing gratitude, which research has shown to be a powerful tool in combating fear and anxiety and building resilience. You'll find new hands-on activities as well as more movement and pair-sharing incorporated into lessons. We hope you will also enjoy new lessons built around Peace of Mind's own story books and skits.

We have also included many more Kindness Pal Activities. Kindness Pals is an important pillar of the Peace of Mind Program that builds classroom community and student connection in powerful ways. We know this is more important than ever as we return to school post-pandemic.

What *Peace of Mind Curriculum* offers is more than simply mindfulness practice or social and emotional skills: we offer an integrated, weekly, year-after-year program that teaches skills for life. Combined with your passion and dedication as a teacher, this is a powerful, transformative combination for our children.

If you find value in teaching *Peace of Mind*, we hope you will share it with your colleagues and friends. Our nonprofit organization, Peace of Mind Inc, exists to be of service to educators who want to bring mindfulness, kindness, and conflict resolution to their students. Please help us spread the word!

Thank you for taking up this important work. Your community and your students need what you have to give.

In peace, Linda and Cheryl
August 2021

Curriculum Overview

Welcome to the *Peace of Mind Core Curriculum for Third Grade*! The Peace of Mind Program helps students develop the skills to notice and manage their emotions; to focus their attention; to practice kindness, empathy and gratitude; to build healthy relationships; and to solve conflicts peacefully – in short, to develop the tools to face life's challenges with compassion and skill.

Teaching the *Peace of Mind Curriculum* weekly over the course of the whole school year, year after year, and integrating elements of *Peace of Mind* into every day life, creates positive change in a classroom and, over time, in school climate, moving schools toward kindness and inclusion.

For an overview of the philosophy, history, and goals of the Peace of Mind Program, please watch the short video introduction by Peace Teacher and curriculum author Linda Ryden on our website: TeachPeaceofMind.org/videos/.

Curriculum Structure

All *Peace of Mind Curricula* include three critical, integrated components:

- Mindfulness
- Brain Science
- Social and Emotional Learning (SEL) with an emphasis on kindness, gratitude, and conflict resolution.

Every lesson begins with Mindfulness Practice. Brain science, social emotional learning (SEL), and conflict resolution lessons are particularly effective because they are built upon this foundation.

Mindfulness in this Curriculum is the practice of paying attention to our thoughts, our feelings, and what is happening around us, and putting some space between our reactions and our response. Mindfulness practice might include quietly sitting to focus on breath awareness, practicing mindful listening, noticing how our bodies feel when we have different emotions, engaging in active movement, and more.

Mindfulness practice is becoming more prevalent in schools because research shows that mindfulness training can help to enhance children's attention and focus (Zenner et al., 2014; Zoogman et al. 2015), improve self-control and emotion regulation (Metz et al., 2013), and improve overall social emotional competence including increased empathy, perspective-taking, and emotional control, and less peer-rated aggression (Schonert-Reichl et al., 2014; Schonert-Reichl & Lawlor, 2010).

Brain science is a key ingredient in *Peace of Mind*'s approach. *Peace of Mind* offers students a basic understanding of the roles of the amygdala, the hippocampus, and the prefrontal cortex in reacting and responding to stimuli. This knowledge helps students understand how and why we get angry, for example, and how and why practicing mindfulness can help us calm down enough to make a decision that moves us closer to the outcome we'd like to have.

Social and Emotional Learning (SEL) is the process through which we learn to manage emotion, set and achieve positive goals, feel and show empathy for others, establish and manage positive relationships, and make responsible decisions (CASEL.org).

A growing body of research shows that tending to students' social and emotional needs has positive benefits. A meta-analysis of 213 school-based SEL programs with over 270,000 students found that students who received SEL instruction, compared to a control group, showed significantly improved social and emotional skills, attitudes and behavior and an 11 percent gain in academic achievement (Durlak et al., 2011).

We are excited about recent research on gratitude which confirms its benefits for social and emotional well-being. According to a white paper produced by the Greater Good Science Center at UC Berkeley for the John Templeton Foundation in 2018, "research suggests that gratitude may be associated with many benefits for individuals, including better physical and psychological health, increased happiness and life satisfaction, decreased materialism, and more."

SEL lessons focus on gratitude and other important topics including kindness, empathy, gratitude, relationship building, inclusion and conflict resolution. Peace of Mind's goals and lesson structure are aligned with the 5 Core Competencies identified by the Collaborative for Social and Emotional Learning (CASEL.org*).*

Conflict Resolution lessons invite students to integrate the mindfulness, brain science, and SEL skills and understandings built over the course of the year. Inspired by the work of William Kreidler of Educators for Social Responsibility, we created **The Conflict C.A.T**. as a way of remembering the three steps to working out a conflict.

C is for Calm Down   This is where students tap into their mindfulness practice.

A is for Apologize   Students can't be involved in an escalating conflict without doing or saying something for which they could apologize.

T is for Toolbox   The Conflict Toolbox is a list of eight ideas to help work things out, such as sharing, taking turns, and compromising.

Peace of Mind teaches Mindfulness-based Social and Emotional Learning.
We know that mindfulness and SEL both have positive benefits for our students and our schools. But here's what's really exciting: we have learned in over a decade of teaching this work to students that integrating mindfulness with SEL is an even more transformative approach than teaching either mindfulness or SEL on its own.

Ultimately, the goal of Peace of Mind is to create a school culture of kindness. Creating a kinder, more positive school climate and dedicating class time for social and emotional learning are two important and evidence-based approaches to bullying prevention (Bradshaw, 2015; O'Brennan & Bradshaw, 2013).

We can't know what challenges our children will face as they grow, but we have confidence that the combination of these internal and external approaches will give students the ability to meet them with skill and compassion.

Lesson Themes

This curriculum is divided into seven sequential units. Through these units, students will build self-awareness and self-regulation skills and develop their ability to build healthy relationships with others. Lessons help students develop individual awareness of their emotions, strengthen their own personal mindfulness practices, and practice compassion and kindness toward themselves. Lessons also help students practice gratitude for others, practice kindness toward others, and solve conflicts peacefully.

Here's how the units flow:

Unit 1: Mindfulness Foundations (5 lessons)

This unit builds a critical foundation for all the lessons that follow, introducing students to a range of mindfulness practices. Students experience the effects of each practice personally and begin or continue (if they have had *Peace of Mind* in younger grades) to discern which practices are most helpful to them.

Unit 2: Gratitude and the Brain's Negativity Bias

In this unit, we explore our brain's tendency to focus on the negative and how gratitude practice helps to balance this tendency by focusing on small good things we experience. Through stories, games, and activities, students experience this for themselves.

Unit 3: Metacognition

In this unit, we help kids begin to learn to notice what they are thinking. We discuss the powerful ideas that we don't have to believe everything that we think and that we have choice in where to focus our attention. Skills for life.

Unit 4: Feelings and Sensations (6 lessons)

In this unit, we explore the embodiment of feelings. When we can notice where feelings begin in our bodies as sensations, we get a head start on gaining control over how we respond to them.

Unit 5: Kindness and Compassion

In this unit, we turn our focus to our relationships with other people. Lessons focus on skills and practices that help us treat others with compassion and kindness. Children experience the benefits of these practices for themselves and others.

Unit 6: Brain Science

In this unit, we review the functions and interrelatedness of three key parts of our brains: the amygdala, the hippocampus, and the prefrontal cortex. Through stories and role plays, students gain powerful insight into themselves and why mindfulness helps us calm down.

Unit 7: Applied Mindfulness: Conflict Resolution

In this unit, we integrate everything we've done until this point. Through stories and role plays, we apply what we've been learning about mindfulness, kindness, empathy, and brain science to the challenge of resolving conflicts peacefully.

End-of-Year Activity

We end with a Kindness Chain as a final way of connecting with each other and appreciating all that we have learned together.

Lesson Sequence

Lessons are designed to be taught in the order in which they are presented. However, we know that in some cases, it may make sense to change the order of lessons to meet your students' needs or to coincide with events in your school community. Please do what you think best meets the needs of your class.

That said, please note that the very first lesson you teach about mindfulness is actually the first step toward peaceful conflict resolution in your classroom. From Week 1, you will be building the foundation that will enable children to solve conflicts with empathy, compassion, and skill. Every lesson is a critical piece of the foundation for successful conflict resolution. Without the foundation, the conflict resolution lessons themselves will be less effective.

All of the lessons bear repeating! If you feel your class needs more practice in a certain area, feel free to repeat a lesson, or segment of the lesson, that feels helpful.

Lesson Framework

Each lesson includes the following components:

- **Mindfulness and Mindfulness Helper**

  Mindfulness is the foundation for everything we teach. Reinforcing each child's ability to be a Mindfulness Helper is important. Helping to lead the class in mindfulness practice supports each child in making the practices their own. Leadership of this part of class may be particularly beneficial for children who do not have leadership opportunities in other areas of their lives. You'll find more on the Mindfulness Helper in the next section.

- **Lesson**

  Weekly lessons are designed to be engaging and fun with a balance of listening, discussion, and activity. Some lessons focus primarily on introducing a new mindfulness practice; most start with a mindfulness practice as the foundation for topics described above.

- **Storybooks and Skits**

  Many lessons use stories to help engage kids in the ideas and skills being taught. Other lessons engage students in acting out stories to help them practice using the skills and tools they are learning, so that they are available to them when they are really needed.

- **Kindness Pals**

  All lessons include a Kindness Pal Activity and close with Kindness Pals. Not only do Kindness Pals give students a way to practice kindness, they are an essential tool for building a positive and inclusive classroom and school community. This practice is described in more detail in the next section.

Preparing to Teach

As you begin to review the curriculum, you will notice that the first paragraph of each lesson offers you an overview of the lesson. All of the lessons offer suggested scripts for you. Please use them as a support, but feel free to teach the lesson in your own words in the way that feels most natural to you.

Once you have read through this guide, it will be helpful to gather materials you will need, spend a little extra time preparing to engage your Mindfulness Helpers and manage Kindness Pals, and take some time for your own mindfulness practice too. Here's what you will need.

Materials

The materials list for *Peace of Mind* is short:

- √ A bell or a chime of some sort that does not have another meaning in your classroom;
- √ Storybooks (see list below).

Optional materials include:

- √ A Talking Object, such as a small stuffed animal or bean bag;
- √ A Hoberman Sphere (a breathing ball), available at your local toy store or online;
- √ Brainy the Puppet ™ (available at TeachPeaceofMind.org).

This curriculum includes lessons built around three Peace of Mind storybooks (list below), original skits, and drawing/writing opportunity worksheets. All Scripts and Worksheet Templates are found in the Resource Section at the end of the curriculum.

You will need the following storybooks by Linda Ryden. If you do not already have them, you can find them at your favorite online retailer or through TeachPeaceofMind.org/shop/.

Marleigh is Mindful
Rosie's Brain
Sergio Sees the Good

NOTE FROM LINDA: *Sometimes I have not been able to find just the right story for the lessons I have wanted to teach, so I have written my own based on what resonates with my students. I hope your students will enjoy these stories and books as much as my students have.*

Get to Know Two Pillars of Peace of Mind

Before beginning to teach *Peace of Mind*, please familiarize yourself with the two consistent features of every lesson: the Mindfulness Helper and Kindness Pals.

Mindfulness Helper

An important component of the mindfulness portion of the curriculum is a Mindfulness Helper. The Mindfulness Helper is a student who leads the class in mindful breathing to prepare for the lesson of the day. The Mindfulness Helper concept is introduced after basic ideas of mindful bodies, mindful listening, and mindful breathing have been established.

Where "Mindfulness Helper" is indicated you may follow these steps or create your own ritual. The placement of the steps is indicated in each lesson that includes a Mindfulness Helper (MH).

- The teacher consults their alphabetical roll list and chooses a student to be the Mindfulness Helper for the day.
- The teacher encourages the class to offer sign language applause for the person who is chosen that day.
- The MH comes to the front of the class and sits next to the teacher on a chair or on the floor if you are sitting in a circle.
- With the teacher's help the MH says slowly, "Let's get into our mindful bodies…. Let's close our eyes or look down. … Let's take three deep breaths." Always offer the students a choice about keeping their eyes open or closed.
- At this point the teacher will lead the rest of the mindfulness practice as instructed in the lesson.
- The MH rings the bell when the mindfulness practice is complete.
- The teacher then asks the MH to return to their seat.

    You will need to help younger students to remember what to say at the beginning of the year. Repeating the same words each class is important to help students develop a routine to help them begin to practice on their own.

Kindness Pals

Kindness Pals is a very popular activity that achieves several goals:

- To remind the children to make kindness part of their daily lives. Doing kind things for their Kindness Pals spills over into their treatment of others.
- To develop the habit of treating people with kindness through regular practice.
- To give children opportunities to get to know each other and to connect with others whom they might not have gotten along with in the past or whom they think they just don't like.

Here is how it works:

- Each week you assign each student one Kindness Pal. You can pair up the children in advance using the Kindness Pals template (see the Resource Section). Assigning new Kindness Pals sometimes happens during the lesson, and sometimes at the end.
- When children receive the names of their Kindness Pals, emphasize that both pals must say "Okay." **This is very important.** This lets the teacher know that they have heard their assignment and that they know who their Kindness Pals are. Please practice this with your class.
- Please let the class know that this is not a time for them to let the teacher or the class know how they feel about having that Kindness Pal. This avoids hurt feelings and also offers multiple chances to remind the children that they have the power to be kind and the power to hurt people's feelings. It all depends on their choices. This is a powerful lesson.
- Explain to the students that they will each receive one Kindness Pal each week. It is their job to do nice things for their assigned Kindness Pals for the whole week. Some examples of kind behavior might be to get a Pal's snack, stack their chair, or play together at recess.
- The following week, allow children to talk about what they did for their Pal, allowing about 5 minutes for this sharing.
- Optional: Use some sort of Taking Object (a stuffed animal or squishy ball) for the sharing. Toss the object to the first speaker and remind

- everyone that the person holding the object gets to talk and the rest of us get to listen.
- Kindness Pals sharing time is a perfect time to practice mindful listening. It's important to demonstrate how we listen mindfully with our whole bodies. Later in the year you might start to let a child lead the sharing and, if you're using one, toss the talking object to the speakers. They love that.
- Then, assign new Kindness Pals for the week ahead if you haven't already.

Especially at the beginning of the year it can help the children remember who their Kindness Pal is if you give them a little chance to chat or greet each other in a friendly way with a high five or friendly words. Any time that you have extra time at the end of a lesson you can give the children an opportunity to chat with their Kindness Pal about some aspect of the lesson or to share their plans for the weekend, for example.

If you are a classroom teacher, you can use Kindness Pals as partners, field trip buddies, and so on. You might allow time for kids to make cards or other things for their Kindness Pal. If you are a counselor or another teacher visiting a classroom, you can talk to the classroom teacher about integrating Kindness Pals into their routine as well as ways to encourage the children to practice kindness.

If you are in a hybrid or virtual setting, you might have your students send messages to each other in the chat or make little videos saying hello to each other.

NOTE FROM LINDA: All of the lessons have suggestions for Kindness Pal activities. We hope you'll have enough time to include them, but if you run out of time and you are a classroom teacher, you can save them for another time or repeat them throughout the week. You can also substitute activities from other lessons or use your own ideas. Through these activities the children get to know each other, expand their social groups, and remember that it is possible to be kind to someone even if they are not your friend.

Mindfulness for Yourself

It is so important to establish your own mindfulness practice before you attempt to teach it to your students. Just as you would never try to teach Spanish before you learned the language yourself, it is important to begin your own mindfulness practice before bringing these simple but transformative skills to your students. You don't have to be an expert in mindfulness, but it is important to join your students on the journey.

There are so many great resources to help you get started. Ten Percent Happier, Calm, and Headspace are secular, simple, step-by-step mindfulness program apps. There are also dozens of books to help you get started. There are more resources listed in the Resources section.

The Peace of Mind online courses are also designed to help you get started in teaching this curriculum. You can find out more about them at TeachPeaceofMind.org/Educators.

Peace of Mind for Third Graders

Welcome again to your Peace of Mind third grade journey! If your students have already had the *Peace of Mind Core Curriculum for Grades 1 and 2*, some of the practices you will be teaching will be familiar to them. Our intention is that children have a chance to continue practicing their mindfulness, SEL, and Conflict Resolution skills each year, deepening their understanding, increasing their sense of ownership of the practices, and developing such familiarity and ease that they are able to put their skills to work when they are really needed, inside and outside of the classroom.

Teaching Mindfulness to third graders can be very rewarding! Unlike younger students, they are often able to sit for longer periods of time and are able to grasp how mindfulness skills are helpful to them in their daily lives. But they are also still very keen to have fun with movements and their imaginations. Children around this age are very interested in learning about themselves and are open to learning how to become more aware of what is happening in their minds and in their hearts.

As in most *Peace of Mind Curriculums*, many lessons focus on breathing and learning how to use our breath to help us handle our emotions. Mindfulness practice can help children to recognize when they are getting angry and assist them in staying calm. In a calm state, children can use the skills taught in the conflict resolution lessons to work out conflicts peacefully, instead of avoiding them or losing control.

In this curriculum children also will begin to learn more about metacognition — learning more about how their own minds work. We'll also begin to focus outward and think about the world around us and begin to develop an understanding of how we can use our skills to stand up for others and for what we believe in.

Most kids are very open to learning about mindfulness. But if you find that you have to do a little convincing, it can be very helpful to relate mindfulness to sports. Many sports teams and sports stars practice mindfulness regularly to enhance their performance. Talking about how mindfulness practice can help us play better by helping us focus, control our temper, be more of a team player, connect our minds and bodies, and calming our nerves can be very influential to student athletes. This can also be true of music, dance, and just about anything else that your students are interested in. Finding the relevance can be important, especially for older elementary students.

The Social and Emotional Learning (SEL) Lessons in this curriculum focus on the power of words to help or hurt. It is important for children to start to understand how powerful their words can be and how it is impossible to take our words back once they are out of our mouths. Many of these lessons are designed to help children start to be more mindful of what they say to others and to take a moment to consider how their words will make other people feel before speaking.

Goals and Expectations

Keep your expectations reasonable. Some kids have a much easier time sitting quietly than others. Sometimes the kid who is sitting with their eyes wide open, legs jiggling, and fiddling with a pencil—but not talking—during mindfulness practice is doing their very best and is benefiting greatly from the effort. That's okay. The exercises in this curriculum are for the benefit of the children and, as long as it is not preventing other children from practicing, a little wiggling around is okay.

Goals for Third Grade

Upon completion of this curriculum, 3rd graders will be able to:

- Use breathing to help manage challenging emotions, like anger or frustration.
- Be more aware of their thoughts and feelings, especially challenging feelings such as worry and anxiety.
- Use mindfulness to calm themselves and focus their attention.
- Begin to learn about metacognition. Understand that their thoughts do not have to control their actions.
- Understand brain function as it relates to being able to calm oneself.
- Practice the habit of being kind.
- Understand and use the Conflict Resolution Tool Kit to resolve conflicts with friends and siblings at school and at home.

Curriculum At-a-Glance

For every lesson, you will need your Kindness Pals list and a bell or chime. Additional materials needed are listed in the table below.

Unit 1 – Mindfulness Foundations				
Week	**Mindfulness Skill**	**Lesson Objective(s)**	**Additional Materials for Lessons**	**Kindness Pal Activity**
1. Introduction to Mindfulness	Mindful Listening	Introduce the concept of mindfulness and create the foundation for mindfulness practice. Introduce (or reintroduce) Kindness Pals. Establish kindness practice.		Three Questions
2. Mindfulness Listening, Mindful Seeing	Mindful Listening and Mindful Seeing	Practice Mindful Listening. Apply the concept of mindfulness to concrete actions. Practice kindness and introduce talking object (if using one).		Three Questions
3. Four Square Breathing	Four Square Breathing	Introduce another foundational mindfulness exercise. Play the Counting Game. Practice kindness.		Three Questions
4. Create Your Own Breath	Create Your Own Breath	Introduce the concept of mindfulness and create the foundation for mindfulness practice. Have fun with mindful breathing. Students create their own mindfulness practices. Practice kindness.	Create Your Own Breath Worksheet	Three Questions
5. Peaceful Place Visualization	Visualization	Learn the skill of visualization to calm down and focus. Practice kindness.	*Marleigh is Mindful* by Linda Ryden	Draw Your Peaceful Place

Unit 2: Gratitude and the Negativity Bias

Week	Mindfulness Skill	Lesson Objective(s)	Additional Materials for Lessons	Kindness Pal Activity
6. Sergio Sees the Good	Cup of Gratitude	Learn about the Negativity Bias and how we can help our brains remember little good things. Practice kindness.	*Sergio Sees the Good* by Linda Ryden	One good thing, One bad thing
7. Gratitude Marble Game	Gratitude Practice. Choice of Take Five Breathing, Four Square Breathing, or Gravity Hands.	Practice training our brains to notice little good things. Reinforce lessons about the Negativity Bias. Practice kindness.	Little cups (one per student) and marbles or any small object that you have a lot of (5 or so per student)	Gratitude Marble Game
8. Little Good Things	Gratitude Practice	Develop a sense of gratitude for the little things in life. Become more mindful of the good that is always around us. Practice kindness.	"Little Good Things" Worksheet	Ten little good things

Unit 3: Metacognition

Week	Mindfulness Skill	Lesson Objective(s)	Additional Materials for Lessons	Kindness Pal Activity
9. Mindfulness of Thoughts	Mindful Breathing	Practice a fundamental skill of Mindfulness. Practice Counting Breaths. Practice kindness.	My Kindness Pals Favorite Things Worksheet	My Kindness Pal's Favorite Things
10. Thought Catcher	Mindful Movement	Notice when your mind wanders. Practice kindness.	Rules of the "Thought Catcher" Game	Nine Words
11. Time Traveling	Past, Present, or Future	Notice if your thoughts are mostly about the past, the present, or the future. Practice kindness.		Nine Words
12. Keeping Your Focus	Gravity Hands	Practice keeping your focus when surrounded by annoying sounds. Practice kindness.	Noisemakers: scissors, wind-up toy, jar of pencils, a squeaky chair, etc.	Mirror Game
13. Using Mindfulness to Take Care of Anger	Gravity Hands Blooming Breaths	Use Mindful Breathing to manage big emotions. Practice kindness.	Field Day Skit found in Resource Section	Mirror Game

| Unit 4: Feelings, Sensations, and Your Body ||||||
Week	Mindfulness Skill	Lesson Objective(s)	Additional Materials for Lessons	Kindness Pal Activity
14. Body Scan	Flashlight Body Scan	Learn that we can be aware of what is happening in our bodies and begin to relate physical feelings to our emotions. Practice kindness.		Kindness Pal Challenge
15. Tummy Breaths	Take Five Breathing	Learn deep belly breathing to help manage strong emotions. Practice kindness.		Kindness Pal Challenge
16. Squeeze and Release	Squeeze and Release	Learn a practice to help relax the body. Practice kindness.		Kindness Pal Challenge
17. Mindful Eating	Take Five Breathing, Mindful Eating	Apply our Mindfulness skills to our everyday lives. Practice kindness.	Enough raisins for all of your class to have one or two	Nine Words
Unit 5: Kindness and Compassion					
18. Kindness Chain	Blooming Breaths	Show the power of our words to illustrate how one act of kindness can set off a chain of kindness. Practice kindness.		Kindness Pal Challenge
19. Heartfulness	Heartfulness	Use the practice of thinking kind thoughts to increase feelings of compassion and empathy for yourself and others. Practice kindness.	Heartfulness Worksheet	Heartfulness Worksheet Share
20. Empathy	Take Five Breathing, Four Square Breathing, or Gravity Hands	Developing awareness of the feelings of others. Practice kindness.	Copies of the "Should We Let Him Play" Skit found in the Resource Section	Sharing about Inclusion and Exclusion

Unit 6: Brain Science				
Week	**Mindfulness Skill**	**Lesson Objective(s)**	**Materials for Lessons**	**Kindness Pal Activity**
21. Rosie's Brain	Gravity Hands	Learn about how three parts of our brain — the amygdala, hippocampus, and the prefrontal cortex — operate in regulating our emotions and reactions to stimuli. Practice kindness.	*Rosie's Brain* by Linda Ryden. Video of Dr. Daniel Siegel's Hand Model of the Brain http://www.drdansiegel.com/resources/everyd ay_mindsight_tools. Diagram of the brain. Brainy the Puppet (Optional)	Kindness Pal Challenge
22. Helping Amy: Amygdala	Choice: Take Five Breathing, Gravity Hands, Four Square Breathing	Learn about how three parts of our brain — the amygdala, hippocampus, and the prefrontal cortex — operate in regulating our emotions and reactions to stimuli. Practice kindness.	Video of Dr. Daniel Siegel's Hand Model of the Brain http://www.drdansiegel.com/resources/everyday_mindsight_tools. Diagram of the brain.	Kindness Pal Sharing
23. Who's the Boss? Prefrontal Cortex	Choice: Take Five Breathing, Gravity Hands, Four Square Breathing	Learn about how three parts of our brain — the amygdala, hippocampus, and the prefrontal cortex — operate in regulating our emotions and reactions to stimuli. Practice kindness.	Diagram of the brain	Mirror Game
24. Do You Remember? Hippocampus	Choice: Take Five	Learn about how three parts of our brain — the amygdala, hippocampus, and the prefrontal cortex — operate in regulating our emotions and reactions to stimuli. Practice kindness.	Copies of *Rosie's Brain* Skit	Hippocampus Workout

Unit 7: Conflict Resolution				
Week	Mindfulness Skill	Lesson Objective(s)	Materials for Lessons	Kindness Pal Activity
25: Learn about conflict with Zion and Zuri	Squeeze and Release	Learn what conflict means. Practice kindness.	*Fun Saturday* by Linda Ryden (in lesson)	Hippocampus Workout
26. The Conflict Escalator	Take Five Breathing	Use the concept of a Conflict Escalator, developed and named by William Kreidler, to help children understand how and why conflicts get worse. Practice kindess.	Copies of the Scrabble vs. Monopoly Skits	Gratitude Marble Game
27. Conflict Escalator Practice: The Class Party	Heartfulness Gravity Hands	Reinforce the concept of the Conflict Escalator and lay the foundation for the Conflict C.A.T. Practice kindness.	Copies of the skits The Class Party 1 and The Class Party 2	Nine Words
28. MOFL or Awful?	Guided Reflection	Understand what makes a good apology. Practice apologizing. Practice kindness.		Kindness Pal Challenge
29. The Conflict C.A.T.	Blooming Breaths	Introduce a new Conflict Resolution method. Practice kindness.	Copy of the Conflict C.A.T. for the classroom	Kindness Pal Challenge
30. The Conflict Toolbox	Your Choice	Introduce more tools to help work out conflicts. Practice kindness.	Copies of the Monopoly vs Scrabble 1 Skit	The Mirror Game
31. Conflict C.A.T. Role Play 1	Body Scan	Practice the Conflict Resolution skills taught in previous lessons. Practice kindness.	Copy Conflict C.A.T. Role Play Scenarios. Have poster of the Conflict Escalator, the Conflict C.A.T., and the Toolbox up for students to see.	Three Questions

Unit 7: Conflict Resolution, continued					
Week	Mindfulness Skill	Lesson Objective(s)	Materials for Lessons	Kindness Pal Activity
32. Conflict C.A.T. Role Play 2	Cup of Gratitude	Reinforce the Conflict C.A.T. through role playing. Practice kindness.	Have poster of the Conflict Escalator, the Conflict C.A.T., and the Toolbox up for students to see.	You choose the Kindness Pal Activity
Year-end Activity					
33. Kindest Things	Heartfulness	Encourage the children to see the good in each other and experience the good feeling of sharing heartfelt compliments. Practice kindness.	Paper, pen, or pencil for every student	Kindest Things

Unit 1: Lessons

Week 1
Introduction to Mindfulness

MINDFULNESS PRACTICE: Mindful Listening

OBJECTIVES: Introduce the concept of mindfulness and create the foundation for mindfulness practice

Introduce (or reintroduce) Kindness Pals

PREPARE: A bell or chime

Your Kindness Pals list

Optional: Talking Object

Welcome to the first lesson of your Peace of Mind third grade journey! Today we'll be introducing the concept of mindfulness. If your students have already had the *Peace of Mind Core Curriculum for Grades 1 and 2*, they may already be familiar with it and you can treat this lesson as a review. Over the next few lessons, we will be teaching kids a variety of mindfulness practices so that they can experience them and learn what works best for them. If they are already familiar with the practices, these lessons will give students a chance to deepen their understanding and build their skill.

Mindfulness Practice

1. **Introduce Mindfulness**

   Say: *Today we are going to start learning about something new together [or reviewing]. It's called mindfulness.*

   Mindfulness is fun because anyone can do it, you can do it anywhere, and you have everything you need to do it right in your own body. You have probably tried it already and didn't even know it.

   Mindfulness is about noticing things. Sometimes we'll notice things by listening or seeing or even by sitting quietly with our eyes closed. You practice mindfulness while you are moving. You can even practice it while you are eating. Are you ready to start?

   The first thing we are going to do is listen.

I'd like you to close or cover your eyes and I'm going to set a timer for thirty seconds. During that time I want you to count inside your mind, not out loud, how many different sounds you hear.

Try not to make any sounds yourself, just sit really still and count the sounds you hear. You might have to listen really hard to hear things. Ready? Close your eyes or look down. Okay let's start listening now…

Wait about thirty seconds or longer if they seem to have an easy time staying still. You might subtly add some sounds (chair squeaking, footsteps, keys softly jingling, etc.) if the room is really quiet.

Say: *Now let's open our eyes.*

2. **Discuss**

    Leave plenty of time for sharing. You might use these kinds of questions to frame a discussion:

    - Who would like to tell us about a sound that you heard?
    - How did you know it was a door squeaking if you couldn't see the door?

    Try to hear from everyone, even if they are sharing about a sound that had already been mentioned.

    If you are short on time, have them share with an elbow partner instead.

    You might say:

    Isn't it interesting how many different sounds we could hear?

    All of these sounds were all around us and yet we weren't paying attention to them.

    This is something you can try anytime—when you are at home, or in the car, or outside on the playground. Just stop and take a moment to do some mindful listening.

3. **Introduce Mindful Bodies**

    Say: *We are going to practice being mindful every time we meet. Whenever we do our mindfulness we are going to get into a special position called a Mindful Body.*

Guide the children into their Mindful Bodies.

If you have the space, resources, and time, it is wonderful to have everyone sitting on the floor on a rug, carpet squares, or little cushions.

If the students are at their desks, ask them to turn their chairs toward the front of the room or move a bit away from their desks in order to reduce distractions.

Ask them to sit up nice and straight, feet on the floor if they reach, and put their hands in their laps.

Practice getting into Mindful Bodies a few times.

Ask the children to feel the difference between the way we normally sit and the way we sit when we are ready to be mindful.

Talk about what it means to be "ready" and how this relates to other activities they may participate in.

Ask the students to describe the "ready position" for the batter in a baseball game, for a soccer goalie, or for a tennis player waiting to return a serve.

Ask: How do children on the playground get into "ready position" before a race or before beginning to jump rope?

Ask: How does a musician or a dancer get their body into position so that they are ready to play or perform?

Then you might say:

In the "ready position," you have noticed that your feet might be still, your body might be in one particular position that's best for the activity you are about to start, and your mind is focused and alert. All of these are to help you do the best you can do in the sport or game or performance ahead. The same is true for mindfulness practice. We get into our Mindful Bodies so that we are in the best possible ready position to be able to use our mindfulness practice to calm ourselves and improve our focus and attention.

> **NOTE FROM LINDA:** *Don't stress about having all kids get into picture perfect mindful bodies! Very few kids will actually stay in their mindful bodies for long if at all. Inviting them to get into their Mindful Bodies is a helpful way to make a transition into what you are doing and to help them practice for the future. If a child is sitting with their eyes wide open, that's fine. I usually ask the kids not to look at each other to give everyone a little privacy. For some kids closing their eyes can be triggering so it's very important to give kids plenty of options and leeway.*

Activity: Mindful Listening

Ask students to get into their Mindful Bodies.

Ask the students to close their eyes.

Ask them to listen to the bell and raise their hands when they can no longer hear the sound.

Ring the bell for the class.

When the last student has raised their hand, **ask** everyone to open their eyes and discuss what they noticed about the sound.

Ask the students if they were able to keep their minds focused on the sound or if their minds wandered to think about something else.

Assure everyone that it is perfectly normal for our minds to wander. In mindfulness practice we are trying to strengthen the focusing part of our minds.

Kindness Pals

Introduce Kindness Pals as follows:

Now we are going to start something called Kindness Pals. Every time we meet, I am going to give you a Kindness Pal. It will be a different person in your class each time. I'm going to ask you to do something kind for this person between now and the next time we meet. It can be something small like stacking their chair or something bigger like drawing them a picture, making them a card, or playing with them at recess. You can even do more than one thing.

Can you think of other kind things you could do for your Kindness Pal?

Give them time to share.

I have one very important rule about Kindness Pals. Since the whole point of Kindness Pals is to help us practice being kind, I want to make sure that we start out with kindness. So when I tell you who your Kindness Pal is going to be, I want you to say "okay" in a friendly way. Let's try that all together: "Okay!"

When I tell you who your Kindness Pal is, you might feel really happy and excited. Maybe your Kindness Pal is already your really good friend, and it will be really easy to be kind to them.

But sometimes when I tell you who your Kindness Pal is, you might feel differently. You might feel a little nervous or shy. And that's fine. Any way that you feel is fine. But in that moment I want you to try really hard to be kind to your Pal and say a nice, friendly "Okay!" That way your Pal will know that you are ready to show them some kindness.

You don't have to become friends with your Pal (although you might), and you don't even have to like your Pal. All I'm asking you to do is to find some way to be kind to them this week.

When we meet next time, I'm going to ask you to try to remember something that you did for your Kindness Pal and share it with the class. Are you ready to find out who your Kindness Pal is?

Read through the list, saying, for example, "Rosie and Henry are Kindness Pals."

Wait for the "Okay" before moving on.

 Kindness Pals Activity: Three Questions

Say: *Now that you know who your Kindness Pal is, we're going to find out a little more about them. Who can think of a question that we could ask our Kindness Pal?*

Listen to students' suggestions. They might suggest asking about their favorite color or favorite food or sport.

Choose three questions.

Ask the students to sit with their Kindness Pals and have a little chat about these questions.

Share. If you have time, you can come back together as a group and ask them to share something that they learned about their Kindness Pals. This exercise is a great way to practice Mindful Listening and help them to develop an interest in others.

Say: *Okay, so now we've gotten to know our Kindness Pal a little better. I can't wait until next time when we get to hear about the kind things you did for your Pal. Have fun!*

Closing words: *Thanks for a great class, everyone. Let's have a nice quiet moment with the bell. You can close your eyes or leave them open but let's sit quietly and listen to the bell. If you want to, you can think about your new Kindness Pal and imagine yourself doing something kind for them.*

Ring the bell or chime.

Week 2
Mindful Listening, Mindful Seeing

MINDFULNESS PRACTICE: Mindful Listening, Mindful Seeing, and Take Five Breathing

OBJECTIVES: Apply the concept of mindfulness to concrete actions

Practice kindness and introduce talking object

PREPARE: A bell or chime

Your Kindness Pals list

Optional: Talking Object

Today we introduce the practice of Take Five Breathing, one of the most beloved practices among Peace of Mind students. If students are already familiar with this practice, you might invite one to demonstrate it for the class as a reminder or introduction for others. This is an option for any of the practices in this curriculum that some students may be familiar with from previous years.

Take Five helps students focus on taking five deep breaths while tracing the fingers of one hand. This practice helps children to reconnect with their bodies and to calm the nervous system. It is one of many practices that allow children to take a pause, allowing them to decide how they want to respond in a situation that causes big emotions.

Mindfulness Practice

1. **Review and reinforce the Mindful Listening exercise from the previous class period. You might say:**

    Today we are going to practice Mindful Listening again. Remember last week when we listened to the bell and raised our hands when we could no longer hear the sound?

    Let's try that again. Do you remember how to get into your Mindful Bodies?

    Repeat exercise from Lesson 1. Ask:

- Was this any different for you this time?
- Did the bell sound the same or different? What else did you notice?
- Was it easier or harder to keep your mind focused on the sound of the bell?

2. Practice Mindful Seeing

Say: *Today we are going to see what we can notice with our eyes if we are really being mindful, if we are really paying attention. I want you to each choose a shape. Raise your hand when you have chosen your shape.*

Let some children share their shape choice.

Say: *When I say "Go," I'm going to ask you to turn off your voice and walk around the room and count in your head how many times you see your shape.*

When I ring the bell it will be time to come back to our seats.

Give them a couple of minutes to do this activity depending on how long they are able to hold their concentration.

Ring the bell.

Share: You can give them a chance to share with the class how many times they saw their shape, or they can share with an elbow partner or with their Kindness Pal.

Say: *Was anybody surprised by how many times you saw your shape? Isn't it amazing how many different shapes are in this room?*

Do you think you could try Mindfully Seeing anywhere else? At home? On your way to school?

Take a few answers.

Variations: You can try this exercise in a variety of ways. You can have them look for letters, numbers, colors, and so on.

3. Introduce Take Five Breathing

Take Five is a nice way to help children calm themselves down when they are upset or need a break. Here's a sample script to use to introduce the concept.

You might say: *Today we're going to practice another way of using our mindful breathing. You might already have learned this one, but it's such a helpful practice that we're going to practice it again.*

Ask: *Has anyone ever heard someone say "Take Five"?*

Take Five means to take a break—usually they mean a five-minute break. We are going to use Take Five in a different way. Hold up your hand like you are going to give someone a high five with your palm facing out and your fingers spread wide.

Now take the index finger of your other hand and trace the outline of your hand. What does it feel like when your finger runs between your fingers? Maybe it's a little tickly?

We're going to do this again, but this time we are going to breathe in when we are tracing up and breathe out when we are tracing down. Starting with your index finger down by your wrist, on the outside of your thumb, trace up your thumb slowly. As you trace up, breathe in, and as you trace down the inside of your thumb, slowly breathe out.

Repeat this motion with all of your fingers until you are back down at your wrist on the outside of your pinky finger. At this point you will have taken five deep breaths.

Take Five is a great way to help you calm down, anytime you need a break. See if you can try it a few times this week.

4. Introduce Mindfulness Helper

Say: *Today I am going to ask someone to be my Mindfulness Helper. This person will help to set us up and lead us as we practice our Mindfulness. I am going to go through our class list alphabetically* (or however you choose to do it). *Everyone will have a turn.*

Consult your alphabetical roll list and choose the first student to be the Mindfulness Helper for the day.

Invite today's Mindfulness Helper (MH) to come to the front of the class to sit next to you on a chair (or next to you on the floor).

Say: *Let's all be happy for _____. (sign language applause)*

Prompt the MH to say: "Let's get into our mindful bodies."

Review what mindful bodies look like.

Prompt the MH to say: "Let's close our eyes or look down."

Say: If you don't feel comfortable closing your eyes you can look straight down into your lap.

Note: Don't worry if some of the children don't close their eyes.

Prompt the MH to say: "Let's do our Take Five Breathing."

Say: *Let's take some nice gentle deep breaths while we trace our hands. When you trace up your finger, breathe in slowly through your nose. When you trace down, breathe slowly out through your mouth. Try to make your breathing so quiet that only you can hear it.*

Now put your hand on your belly and try to make the rest of your body so still and quiet that the only thing that you feel moving is your breath. Notice what you feel there.

Now, let's all listen with your eyes closed or looking down into your lap as the Mindfulness Helper rings the bell. Try to listen to the whole sound of the bell. Open your eyes or look up when you can't hear it anymore.

Ask the MH to ring the bell and return to their seat.

Ask: *How did it feel to do your Take Five Breathing?*

Note: Repeating the same or similar words each class will help to establish a routine that will help the children to practice on their own. With younger students, it will take some time to establish the practice. Be patient with it and it will become a nice structure for starting the class.

> NOTE FROM LINDA: *The Mindfulness Helper becomes quite a coveted position in each class and sometimes the children are disappointed when it is not their turn. I like to encourage the children to be happy for each other, so I ask them to do sign language applause (wave both hands by the side of your head) when the Mindfulness Helper is chosen.*
>
> *I use this as a teachable moment to help the kids learn that you can choose how you respond to your situation. I remind them that you can choose to be upset every time someone else is chosen, but that means that you will be upset almost every time. Or you can choose to be happy for everyone who is chosen, and then you will be happy every time. Every time I choose the MH I say, "Let's be happy for _____" and for the most part they all join in and feel good. It makes the MH feel good, and that good feeling seems to spread. I also use this method when I choose children to act out the stories in the curriculum. This is a good time to remind your students that we often have more than one emotion at the same time and it can be helpful to notice that. We can be happy for someone else and disappointed for ourselves in the same moment.*

Kindness Pals

You might begin by saying: *Last time we met I gave you a Kindness Pal and asked you to do something kind for them. Did anybody remember to do something for their Pal?*

Who would like to share what you did?

I'm going to [pass the talking object to/ call on] someone who is ready to share.

Don't worry if the kids don't remember to do anything for their Kindness Pal. This might take practice and some gentle reminders.

You might choose to use a talking object to identify whose turn it is to talk. For some classes this can be a helpful way of keeping the other kids focused on the speaker. If it's a distraction or not necessary for your group, feel free not to use it.

If using the talking object, say: *When you are holding the talking object, it is your turn to share. If you are not holding the talking object, it is your turn to listen.*

If you are not using the talking object, be sure to remind your students to really listen to each other. This is such an important life skill and there are so many opportunities to practice it in these lessons.

Call on someone or pass the talking object to someone to speak; they can then pass the turn to their Kindness Pal, who can either share what they did or say "thank you" to their Pal. This little practice helps the children to develop a sense of gratitude for little kindnesses.

Assign new Kindness Pals after they are finished sharing.

Kindness Pal Activity: Three Questions

Say: *Now that you know who your Kindness Pal is, we're going to find out a little more about them. Let's ask our Kindness Pal three questions like we did last time. Who can think of a question that we could ask our Kindness Pal?*

Listen to students' suggestions. They might suggest asking about their favorite color or favorite food or sport.

Choose three questions.

Ask the students to sit with their Kindness Pals and have a little chat.

Share. If you have time, you can come back together as a group and ask them to share something that they learned about their Kindness Pals. This exercise is a great way to practice Mindful Listening and help them to develop an interest in others.

Say: *Okay, so now we've gotten to know our Kindness Pal a little better. I can't wait until next time when we get to hear about the kind things you did for your Pal. Have fun!*

Closing words: *Our time is up for today. Thank you for a great class, everyone.*

Let's have a nice quiet moment for the bell. If you want to, you can close your eyes, picture your new Kindness Pal, and imagine yourself doing something kind for him or her this week.

Ring the bell.

Week 3
Four Square Breathing

MINDFULNESS PRACTICE: Four Square Breathing

OBJECTIVES: Introduce another foundational mindfulness exercise

Play the Counting Game

Practice kindness

PREPARE: A bell or chime

Your Kindness Pals list

Optional: Talking Object

This week, we will introduce yet another mindful breathing practice. Our goal here is not to ensure children master each one, but to help them experience a range of practices so that they can find the one that works best for them. Ultimately, we want children to feel that these tools belong to them and are available to them whenever they are needed, inside or outside of the classroom.

We all benefit from reminders of the tools available to us. Peace of Mind has developed a "Ways to Practice Mindfulness" Poster for the classroom that has colorful illustrations of 9 different practices you will be teaching. You can check it out at TeachPeaceofMind.org.

Our most recent book, *Marleigh is Mindful*, is another helpful resource. This "mindfulness how-to guide for kids" can be a helpful companion to this curriculum. On each page a child talks about a particular challenge or challenging emotion and then teaches a mindfulness practice, such as Four Square Breathing, that can help with that challenge. We don't include specific lessons using *Marleigh is Mindful* in this curriculum (you can find some in the *Peace of Mind Core Curriculum for Grades 1 & 2*) but you are welcome to use the book to support you in teaching this curriculum. It can be a great book to have on your bookshelf or to use to illustrate some of the practices.

Mindfulness Practice

1. **Introduce mindful breathing to the class**

   You might say:

   Today we are going to talk about breathing. Breathing is something you do all day and night, but you hardly ever think about it. When are some times that you might be more aware or mindful of your breath?

   Allow children to answer. Their responses will likely be along the lines of: when you are "out of breath" after a big run, when you are angry and breathing hard, and so on.

2. **Lead the class in a mindful breathing exercise. You might say:**

   Remember last time we learned Take Five Breathing? We traced our hands up and down and breathed slowly in and out. Let's try that again (do Take Five breathing). There are lots of different ways of being mindful of your breathing and we'll learn lots of ways of using our mindful breathing to help us to calm down, focus, work out problems, and lots of other things.

3. **Introduce Four Square Breathing**

   Today we're going to learn something called **Four Square Breathing**. *This is a way of paying attention to our breath and to the spaces between our breaths. Take a few deep breaths and see if you can notice the little tiny moment between your in-breath and your out-breath.* (Let them try that a few times.)

   You might say: *When I was a kid we used to play a game called Four Square at recess. Do any of you play it? This is a little different.*

   Show the video if you choose: (https://TeachPeaceofMind.org/students-2/)

   Say: *Four Square Breathing is another fun way to take deep breaths to help you to calm down. To do Four Square Breathing, draw an invisible square in the air in front of you. Imagine that you are starting in the bottom left-hand corner of your square. As you breathe in you draw a line up while you slowly count to four. Then you hold your breath as you draw a line across the top and slowly count to four. Then you breathe out as you draw a line down and slowly count to four. Then you wait as you draw a line across the bottom connecting the lines of the square and slowly count to four.*

Say: *Let's try it!* Try it a couple of times.

Consult your alphabetical roll list, and choose the first student to be the Mindfulness Helper for the day.

Invite today's Mindfulness Helper (MH) to come to the front of the class to sit next to you on a chair (or next to you on the floor).

Say: *Let's all be happy for _____.* (sign language applause)

Prompt the MH to say: "Let's get into our mindful bodies."

Review what mindful bodies look like.

Prompt the MH to say: "Let's close our eyes or look down."

Say: *If you don't feel comfortable closing your eyes, you can look straight down into your lap.*

Note: Don't worry if some of the children don't close their eyes.

Prompt the MH to say: "Let's do our Four Square Breathing."

Say: *Let's get ready to trace that square in the air in front of us. As you draw a line up the side you will breathe in, as you draw a line across you will hold your breath, as you draw a line down you will breathe slowly out, and as you draw the line across the bottom to close the square you will wait and slowly count to four.*

Now you can begin drawing the lines and say:

Breathe in 2,3,4 (drawing line up)

Hold your breath 2,3,4 (drawing line across the top)

Breathe gently out 2,3,4 (drawing line down the side)

And now wait 2,3,4 (drawing the line across the bottom)

Repeat two or three times.

Now, let's all listen with your eyes closed or looking down into your lap as the Mindfulness Helper rings the bell. Try to listen to the whole sound of the bell. Open your eyes or look up when you can't hear it anymore.

Ask the MH to ring the bell and return to their seat.

Ask students to open their eyes and share what they noticed about their breath.

Activity: The Counting Game

This is a fun Mindfulness game that is sometimes used in theater classes. It works here nicely because it teaches the children to listen mindfully, to focus completely on a task, to be patient with one another, and to work together as a team.

Start out with the kids sitting close together if possible. Tell everyone that they are going to try to count to ten as a group.

You might use this script to introduce the game and provide guidance:

Today we are going to try to count to ten as a group. That sounds easy but it's actually pretty hard.

We are going to close our eyes and listen carefully.

At some point one of you will say "one" and then someone else will say "two" and we'll keep going until we get to ten.

The challenge is that every time I hear two of you say a number at the same time, you'll have to start all over again.

To make the game work, you are going to have to listen very carefully to each other.

You are also going to have to be mindful of not taking too many turns.

You also have to be mindful of making sure that you participate.

If we get to ten, we can keep going.

To start things out, I will say, "Start and go." Every time I hear two of you say a number at the same time I will say, "Start again and go."

Please don't make a lot of noise when that happens. Just take a deep breath and start over again. Ready to try it?

This game is harder than it sounds! Encourage the children to be patient and kind with each other. There will of course be kids who want to say all the numbers who might need gentle reminders not to dominate the game, and there will also be those too afraid to chime in who will need encouragement.

Kindness Pals

Invite the children to share what they have done for their Kindness Pals as described in Week 1.

Assign new Kindness Pals after they are finished sharing.

 ### Kindness Pal Activity: Three Questions

Say: *Now that you know who your Kindness Pal is, we're going to find out a little more about them. Let's think of three questions to ask our Kindness Pal again. Who can think of a question that we could ask our Kindness Pal?*

Listen to students' suggestions. They might suggest asking about their favorite color or favorite food or sport.

Choose three questions.

Ask the students to sit with their Kindness Pals and have a little chat.

Share. If you have time, you can come back together as a group and ask them to share something that they learned about their Kindness Pals. This exercise is a great way to practice Mindful Listening and help them to develop an interest in others.

Say: *Okay, so now we've gotten to know our Kindness Pal a little better. I can't wait until next time when we get to hear about the kind things you did for your Pal. Have fun!*

Closing words: *Our time is up for today. Thank you for a great class, everyone.*

Let's have a nice quiet moment for the bell. If you want to, you can close your eyes, picture your new Kindness Pal, and imagine yourself doing something kind for them this week.

Ring the bell.

Week 4
Create Your Own Breath

MINDFULNESS PRACTICE: Create Your Own Breath

OBJECTIVES: Introduce the concept of mindfulness and create the foundation for mindfulness practice.

Have fun with mindful breathing.

Students create their own mindfulness practices.

Practice kindness.

PREPARE: A bell or chime

Create Your Own Breath Worksheet

Your Kindness Pals list

Optional: Talking Object

Today we introduce the concept of Mindful Movements and invite students to create their own mindful breathing practices. Mindfulness does not necessarily require sitting quietly with eyes closed. Our goal is to help students experience mindfulness as their own practice from the very beginning. Some students will find breathing practices help them most; others will notice that adding movement really helps to calm their nervous system. As always, we will be guiding students to notice what works best for them.

Mindfulness Practice

1. Introduce the lesson

You might say: *So far we have practiced Mindful Listening, Mindful Seeing, Take Five Breathing, and Four Square Breathing. There are a lot more ways to do mindful breathing that we'll learn later. But today we're going to have some fun making up our own ways to take deep breaths. This time we are going to be using our whole bodies to create Mindful Movements to go with our deep breaths. Taking deep breaths is a big part of mindfulness. Deep breaths can* *help us to calm down when we get mad or upset and it feels good. First let's get into our Mindful Bodies and practice Four Square Breathing again!*

2. Practice Four Square Breathing.

Consult your alphabetical roll list and choose the first student to be the Mindfulness Helper for the day.

Invite today's Mindfulness Helper (MH) to come to the front of the class to sit next to you on a chair (or next to you on the floor).

Say: *Let's all be happy for _____.* (sign language applause)

Prompt the MH to say: "Let's get into our mindful bodies."

Review what mindful bodies look like.

Prompt the MH to say: "Let's close our eyes or look down."

Say: *If you don't feel comfortable closing your eyes, you can look straight down into your lap.*

Note: Don't worry if some of the children don't close their eyes.

Prompt the MH to say: "Let's do our Four Square Breathing."

Say: *Let's get ready to trace that square in the air in front of us. As you draw a line up the side you will breathe in, as you draw a line across you will hold your breath, as you draw a line down you will breathe slowly out, and as you draw the line across the bottom to close the square you will wait and don't breathe in yet.*

Now you can begin drawing the lines and say:

Breathe in 2,3,4 (drawing line up)

Hold your breath 2,3,4 (drawing line across the top)

Breathe gently out 2,3,4 (drawing line down the side)

And now wait 2,3,4 (drawing the line across the bottom)

Repeat two or three times.

Now, let's all listen with your eyes closed or looking down into your lap as the Mindfulness Helper rings the bell. Try to listen to the whole sound of the bell. Open your eyes or look up when you can't hear it anymore.

Ask the MH to ring the bell and return to their seat.

Activity: Fun with Mindful Breathing

1. **Create Your Own Breath**

   The purpose of this lesson is to get kids used to taking these deep breaths, bring movement into the class, and to have fun. This will lay the foundation for other kinds of mindfulness practices and will give the kids a sense of ownership over their own mindfulness practice in the future.

   You might say*: Like I said earlier, one of the best ways to help us to calm down when we get mad or frustrated is to take some deep breaths. There are lots of ways to do this. Let's see what we can make up right now using our whole bodies!*

   I'll go first. I'm going to do a Mindful Movement and I want you to see if you can guess what it's called.

   Demonstrate by standing up and slowly moving your arms up and down like butterfly wings bending your knees up and down to match your wings. Breathe in when you flap your wings up and breathe out when you flap your wings down. Make the breathing a little exaggerated so that they will get the idea. (Feel free to make up your own here.)

   Take some guesses.

   Say: *That's right - I was doing Butterfly Breaths! Now let's hear your ideas. Your Mindful Movement can be based on anything — animals, sports, musical instruments, nature, your favorite game — just make sure that you are using your whole body.*

   Invite the kids to create their own Mindful Movements and ask a few to share. Encourage everybody to try each idea.

2. **Draw a picture of your Mindful Movement**

   Hand out copies of the Mindful Movements Worksheet.

Invite the students to draw a picture of their own Mindful Movement.

Sending these worksheets home provides a valuable family connection to what children are learning in class.

Kindness Pals

Invite the children to share what they have done for their Kindness Pals as described in Week 1.

Assign new Kindness Pals after they are finished sharing.

 Kindness Pals Activity: Three Questions

If you have time, you can give them time for a "Three Questions" Kindness Pal chat like they had in earlier lessons.

Closing Words: *Our time is up for today. Let's have a nice quiet moment with the bell. You can close your eyes or leave them open, but let's sit quietly and listen to the bell. If you want to, you can think about your new Kindness Pal and imagine yourself doing something kind for them.*

Ring the bell or chime. *Thanks for a great class, everyone.*

Week 5
Peaceful Place Visualization

MINDFULNESS PRACTICE: Visualization

OBJECTIVES: Learn the skill of visualization to calm down and focus

Practice kindness

PREPARE: A bell or chime

Your Kindness Pals list

Optional: Talking Object

Visualization is a fun way to practice mindfulness that the children really enjoy. Focusing your mind on a peaceful place can help you to calm down, to focus your mind, to think about your senses, and to really settle yourself into the moment, even if it is in your imagination.

Please consider the composition of your class when you offer examples of Peaceful Places a student might call to mind. It could be a real place, an imaginary place, a vacation memory, or a local park.

Mindfulness Practice

1. **Introduce the Peaceful Place Practice**

   You might say: *Today our mindfulness practice will be focusing on a peaceful place. Sometimes when things feel overwhelming in the moment, it helps to think about a place that makes you feel peaceful and happy. Let's try it together.*

   Consult your alphabetical roll list, and choose the first student to be the Mindfulness Helper for the day.

   Invite today's Mindfulness Helper (MH) to come to the front of the class to sit next to you on a chair (or next to you on the floor).

   Say: *Let's all be happy for _____.* (sign language applause)

   Prompt the MH to say: "Let's get into our mindful bodies."

Prompt the MH to say: "Let's close our eyes or look down."

2. **Guide the children through a visualization exercise.**

   Here is a script you can use.

   Say: *Today we are going to be thinking about a Peaceful Place. Try to think about a place where you have felt really peaceful. It can be a real place, a place you've been to on vacation, your own backyard, or a place in your imagination.*

   Give them a moment to think.

   Now let's travel to this peaceful place. Take a look around at your Peaceful Place. Are you inside or outside? What is the weather like? What can you see there? Are there trees? Is there water? If you are in a room, what color are the walls? Look around and really try to notice everything that you can see in your Peaceful Place.

   Take another look around and see what you might have missed.

   Pause.

   Now I'd like you to listen closely. What sounds do you hear in your Peaceful Place? Do you hear birds, or the sound of the waves crashing into the shore? Do you hear people talking? Music? What else do you hear?

   Pause.

   What does it smell like in your Peaceful Place? Do you smell salty air? Sunscreen? Freshly cut grass? Cookies baking? What else do you smell in your Peaceful Place?

   Pause.

   What can you feel with your body in your Peaceful Place? Do you feel sand under your feet and between your toes? Do you feel water? Is it cold or warm? Can you feel the sun on your face? Do you feel a soft blanket? What else do you feel in your Peaceful Place?

   Pause.

What does it feel like in your heart to be in your Peaceful Place? What kind of peaceful feeling do you have? Happy, safe, welcome, relaxed? Try to notice how you feel in your heart in your Peaceful Place.

Pause.

Now we are going to travel back to this peaceful place right here in our classroom.

In a moment you will hear the sound of the bells and that will mean that it is time to open your eyes. So just get ready for that.

Ask the MH to ring the bell and return to their seat.

Reflect and Share

Ask some children to share a few details about their Peaceful Places.

Kindness Pals

Invite the children to share what they have done for their Kindness Pals as described in Week 1.

Assign new Kindness Pals after they are finished sharing.

 Kindness Pals Activity: Kindness Pal Challenge

Say: *Now that you have imagined your Peaceful Place you are going to spend a little time with your new Kindness Pal talking about your Peaceful Place and drawing a picture of it. I'm going to pass out the Peaceful Place worksheet and you can draw together while you tell each other about your peaceful places.*

Closing words: *Okay, our time is up for today. Thank you for a great class, everyone. Let's have a nice quiet moment for the bell. If you want to, you can close your eyes, picture your new Kindness Pal, and imagine yourself doing something kind for them this week.*

Ring the bell.

UNIT 2:
Gratitude and The Negativity Bias

Week 6
Sergio Sees the Good

MINDFULNESS PRACTICE: Cup of Gratitude

OBJECTIVES: Learn about the Negativity Bias and how we can help our brains remember little good things.

Practice kindness

PREPARE: A bell or chime

Sergio Sees the Good **by Linda Ryden**

Your Kindness Pals list

Optional: Talking Object

This week we will be talking about a powerful concept: how gratitude practice can balance out our brain's tendency to focus on negative things, known as the negativity bias. Bad things do happen, and often we let them overshadow all of the small good things that also fill our days. By using the gratitude practices in this lesson, we can balance out our perception of our days which can make us feel happier.

In this lesson students will be hearing the story *Sergio Sees the Good*. If your students had the *Peace of Mind Core Curriculum for 1st & 2nd grade* last year, then they will have heard this story before. That's fine! As you know, kids love to hear their favorite stories again and they will understand the brain science in a different way at this age.

Introduction

Ask: *Does anyone have an idea about what the word "gratitude" means?*

Take a few answers.

That's right — it means being grateful or thankful. Today we're going to learn about a way to practice gratitude and we're going to read a book called Sergio Sees the Good.

*We're going to be making a **Cup of Gratitude.** We'll be thinking about people or things that we are grateful for and we'll be imagining that we are putting them in our little cup.*

Can you make a little cup with your hands? Imagine you are going to drink some water and use your hands as a cup — can you do that? Now we're going to be thinking about people, animals, and things that we are grateful or thankful for. We're going to imagine that they are really tiny and can fit into our cupped hands. Let's get started.

Mindfulness Practice

Invite today's Mindfulness Helper (MH) to come to the front of the class to sit next to you on a chair.

Say: *Let's all be happy for _____.* (sign language applause)

Prompt the MH to say: "Let's get into our mindful bodies. Let's close our eyes or look down. Let's take three deep breaths."

Say: *So let's begin:*

Let's start by making our gratitude cups with our hands.

Now try to think about someone at home that you see every day or almost every day that you are thankful or grateful for. Think of someone who helps you and is kind to you. Now imagine that you can hold them in your little Cup of Gratitude.

Now let's take a deep breath in and as you breathe out, whisper "thank you" into your little cup.

Maybe there is a special animal in your life such as a pet or a stuffed animal or an animal in the wild. Imagine that they are in your little Cup of Gratitude. Let's send some thanks to that animal. Take a deep breath in and as you breathe out, whisper "thank you" into your little cup.

Next, let's think about someone in your class who is kind to you. Imagine that they are in your little Cup of Gratitude. Let's send some thanks to that person. Take a deep breath in and as you breathe out, whisper "thank you" into your little cup.

Take a moment to soak in this feeling of gratitude. Notice what it feels like to be grateful and to say thank you. Remember that you can do this practice on your own anytime.

Let's take a deep breath in and stretch your arms up over your head and then slowly float your arms down as you breathe out. Let's listen for the sound of the bell and we'll open our eyes or look up when we can't hear it anymore.

Say: *In a moment you will hear the sound of the bell and that will mean that it is time to open your eyes or look up. So just get ready for that.*

Ask the MH to ring the bell and return to their seat.

Read and Discuss: The Negativity Bias and *Sergio Sees the Good*

Say: *Today we're going to read a book called* Sergio Sees the Good. *This is a book that teaches us about why it's so important to notice the little good things in life. We'll also learn something new about our brains!*

Read *Sergio Sees the Good*

As Sergio's mom adds marbles to their scale, have kids keep track of how many marbles are on each side of the scale. You can ask them to make tally marks on a piece of paper or a white board, or do it on their fingers or in their minds.

Ask:

- Did Sergio really have a completely terrible day?
- What are the little good things that he forgot all about?
- Why do you think Sergio only remembered that one bad thing?

Kindness Pals

Invite the children to share what they have done for their Kindness Pals as described in Week 1.

Assign new Kindness Pals.

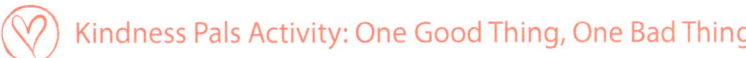 Kindness Pals Activity: One Good Thing, One Bad Thing

Instruct: *Now we're going to sit with our new Kindness Pal and you can each share one good thing and one bad thing that happened to you today.*

Closing Words: *Let's have a nice quiet moment with the bell. You can close your eyes or leave them open, but let's sit quietly and listen to the bell. If you want to, you can think about your new Kindness Pal and imagine yourself doing something kind for him or her.*

Ring the bell or chime. *Thanks for a great class, everyone.*

Week 7
Gratitude Marble Game

MINDFULNESS PRACTICE: Take Five Breathing or Four Square Breathing

Gratitude practice

Objectives: Practice training our brains to notice little good things.

Reinforce lessons about the Negativity Bias.

Practice kindness.

Prepare: A bell or chime

Your Kindness Pals list

Little cups (one for each student) and marbles or pasta, paperclips, any small things that you have a lot of (five or so for each student)

Optional: Talking Object

Today we are going to continue learning about the impact of noticing the little good things using a call and response practice called Tell Me Something Good. We hope you have fun with it! This is a chance to remind your students that by noticing the little good things we're not trying to sweep bad things under the rug or ignore them, but we are trying to make sure that our brains don't convince us that things are worse than they really are. We will refer back to the book we read last week, *Sergio Sees the Good*.

Today we invite kids to choose between two practices they have already learned for today's practice. Offering choice is a trauma-sensitive mindfulness teaching practice, and supports children in their journey of making their practice their own.

Mindfulness Practice

1. Gratitude Practice: Tell Me Something Good

Say: Sometimes it can be easy to forget to notice these little good things in life, so we are going to practice being grateful and mindfully noticing. And to make it even more fun, we are going to sing a little song about it.

I'm going to ask you to think of a little good thing in your life and then raise your hand. When I call on you, we'll all sing "tell me something good" and then you will tell us your good thing. I'll go first. Sing it with me, "tell me something good"! And I'll tell you that I had waffles for breakfast or [Insert your own answer here]. *Now it's your turn.*

Call on whomever raises their hand and **say or sing**: "[Child's Name], tell me something good…" Try to leave enough time for everyone to share. If the kids start to head in the direction of getting things like video games or vacations, remind them to focus on the little good things.

2. **Vote on a Mindfulness Practice**

    Before you begin, ask the class what kind of breathing they would like to practice today. Let them choose between Take Five Breathing and Four Square Breathing. Take a vote. This is a good way to keep them excited about the practice. Allowing students to choose the practice that works best for them is also a trauma-sensitive teaching approach.

    Invite today's Mindfulness Helper (MH) to come to the front of the class to sit next to you on a chair (or next to you on the floor).

    Say: *Let's all be happy for _____.* (sign language applause)

    Prompt the MH to say: "Let's get into our mindful bodies. Let's close our eyes or look down. Let's (insert whatever they decided to do here.)"

    Say: *Now let your breath settle back into its natural rhythm. Just breathe. Put your hand on your belly and try to make your body so still and quiet that the only thing that you can feel moving is your breath.*

    Wait a few moments to see how long they can hold this focus.

    Say: *Now take a deep breath, and listen for the sound of the bell. Try to listen to the whole sound of the bell. Open your eyes when you cannot hear it anymore.*

    Ask the MH to ring the bell and return to their seat.

Activity: Gratitude Marble Game

> NOTE FROM LINDA: *This is one of the most popular activities in my classroom! If you have time you can do this several times throughout the school year!*

In this activity, you will help the children try to remember all of the little good things that happened to Sergio in last week's book *Sergio Sees the Good*. If you have a balance scale you can use that, otherwise just use two cups and some marbles or whatever little objects you have around.

Say: *Today we are going to play a game that will help us to train our brains to notice the little good things. Do you remember in* Sergio Sees the Good *when his mother got out a scale and some marbles and they tried to remember everything that happened to Sergio that day?*

We're going to try to remember all of the good and bad things that happened to Sergio and we're going to put a marble in the good side (or cup) for all the good things and a marble in the bad side (or cup) for all the bad things.

Go through the story with the class and see if they can remember what happened.

Say: *Do you remember that Sergio told his mom that he had a totally terrible day? Was he right? That's right — he had forgotten about most of the good things that happened. His brain was really focused on the one bad thing that happened and that was all that he was remembering.*

Kindness Pals

Say: *Now you're going to get a chance to try it!*

Assign new Kindness Pals. First I'm going to tell you who your new Kindness Pal is. If we have time at the end, you will be able to share what you did for your pals last week.

Assign new Kindness Pals.

♡ Kindness Pal Activity: Gratitude Marble Game

Say: *Now I'm going to give you and your Kindness Pal two cups and some marbles (or pasta, paperclips, whatever you have). You are going to sit across from each other with the cups in between you. You can choose one cup to be the Good cup and one cup to be the Bad cup.*

Then you are going to decide who goes first. That person will be the talker and the other person will hold the marbles. The talker will try to remember everything that happened yesterday and the marble holder will put marbles in the good cup for good things and in the bad cup for bad things. At the end you can count how many marbles are in each cup. Then you will switch places. Try to remember lots of little details.

Give them about 5-10 minutes for this. This is a powerful practice because not only are they thinking about and remembering little good things but they are really listening to each other and witnessing each other's lives.

When the time is up, ask the kids to reflect on how many good and bad marbles they had in each cup and what it felt like to do the activity.

If you have time, give students time to share what they did for their previous kindness pals over the last week.

Closing Words: *Let's have a nice quiet moment with the bell. You can close your eyes or leave them open, but let's sit quietly and listen to the bell. If you want to, you can think about your new Kindness Pal and imagine yourself doing something kind for him or her.*

Ring the bell or chime. *Thanks for a great class, everyone.*

Week 8
Little Good Things

MINDFULNESS PRACTICE: Gratitude Practice

OBJECTIVES: Develop a sense of gratitude for the little things in life.

Become more mindful of the good that is always around us.

Practice kindness.

PREPARE: A bell or chime

The "Little Good Things" Worksheet

Your Kindness Pals list

Optional: Talking Object

In this lesson we emphasize the practice we introduced in the previous lesson of focusing on the small good things in our days, not just the frustrating, sad or bad things that happen to us. We'll talk about the science that shows that practicing gratitude can help us maintain a more balanced sense of our days.

Mindfulness Practice

Invite today's Mindfulness Helper (MH) to come to the front of the class to sit next to you on a chair.

Say: Let's all be happy for _____. (sign language applause)

Prompt the MH to say: "Let's get into our mindful bodies. Let's close our eyes or look down. Let's take three deep breaths."

Say: Today we are going to be thinking about gratitude or being thankful. I'd like you to think about that word "gratitude." I'd like you to ask yourself a question: "What or who am I grateful or thankful for right now?"

Don't think about it too much but just notice what pops into your mind. Maybe you are grateful that it's almost time for recess, or that it isn't raining today, or that you have your favorite lunch waiting for you. Maybe you're thankful for *having shoes that fit, socks that aren't itchy, or having a friend to laugh with. Whatever it is that pops into your mind, just notice it.*

Say: *Now take a deep breath, and listen for the sound of the bell. When you hear that sound it will be time to open your eyes.*

Ask the MH to ring the bell and return to their seat.

Gratitude Practice

Say: *Today we are going to be thinking about gratitude. Sometimes when we think about being thankful or grateful, we think about big things. Maybe you are grateful to have a home, or a family, or the chance to go to school. It's really important to appreciate those things.*

There are also a million little things that we can be grateful for if we just stop to notice them. I'm thinking about really little things like the smell of crayons, or the way the cheese sometimes stretches really far from your mouth to the pizza, or the sound of a baby laughing. (Feel free to replace these with your own examples!)

Ask the students to share their own little good things.

Share some science: *Scientists who study brains have learned that one way to overcome the Negativity Bias is to focus on little good things rather than just big things like family or friends or health. If we notice these little good things and — this is important — take a few moments to savor them to remember the little details about how things smell or sound or feel or how we felt when we noticed those little good things, our brains can store those memories in long-term storage.*

The more we do this, the better our brains get at noticing and remembering the little good things. Since our brains are so good at remembering and storing negative memories, this practice gives us a chance to balance out the bad with the good.

As always, we're not trying to pretend that bad things don't happen — we just don't want our brains to trick us into thinking that good things aren't happening too!

You may choose to start a classroom list of little good things that the students can add to every day.

Kindness Pals

Invite the children to share what they have done for their Kindness Pals as described in Week 1.

Assign new Kindness Pals.

 Kindness Pal Activity

Say: *Now I'm going to give you your new Kindness Pal and you two are going to work together to come up with a list of* **Ten Little Good Things**. *When everybody is done we'll share some of what is on our lists. At the end of this activity, you will be able to share what you did for your Kindness Pals over the last week.*

Assign new Kindness Pals.

Hand out the Ten Little Good Things Worksheet.

Give them about ten minutes to work on it and then time to share.

Closing words: *Okay our time is up for today. Thank you for a great class, everyone.*

Let's have a nice quiet moment for the bell. If you want to, you can close your eyes, picture your new Kindness Pal, and imagine yourself doing something kind for them this week.

Ring the bell.

Additional Gratitude Activities

If you feel your students would benefit from additional gratitude practice, here are two more options to consider.

1. **"Brush Up On Gratitude!"**

    Do a classroom gratitude challenge. Every time you brush your teeth, think of three things you are grateful for. Make a big class chart and see how many different things you can get. Maybe challenge another class?

2. **Classroom Gratefuls Box**

    Decorate a tissue box or any kind of container and keep sticky notes and pencils nearby. Ask the students to write down any little good things that they feel grateful for and put them in the box. Once a week during Morning Meeting or anytime, have the class read them out loud.

UNIT 3:
Metacognition:
Mindfulness of Thoughts

Week 9
Mindfulness of Thoughts

MINDFULNESS PRACTICE: Mindful Breathing

OBJECTIVES: Practice a fundamental skill of Mindfulness.

Practice Counting Breaths.

Practice kindness.

PREPARE: A bell or chime

Kindness Pals list

Copies of My Kindness Pals Favorite Things Worksheet (See Resource Section)

Optional: Talking Object

In this unit, we are turning our attention to noticing our thoughts. Metacognition, or thinking about thinking, is a powerful tool to help us develop self-awareness. Through mindfulness practices such as the one we will do today, we learn to notice where we tend to focus our thoughts and to gain control over how we direct our attention. We start here with a mindful breathing practice called "Count Ten Breaths" that prompts students to notice when their attention has wandered and then bring it back to focus on their breathing. Having our minds wander is completely normal; being able to bring our attention back to where we would like it to be is a skill we can develop and strengthen.

Mindfulness Practice

1. **Introduce the Practice**

    You might say: *Today we are going to continue practicing mindful breathing. Let's do a few of our own Mindful Movements to get us started. Do you remember some of the Mindful Movements we've done before? Let's think of some new ones!*

    Do a few of their Mindful Movements.

    Say: *Today we are going to be focusing on our breath in a new way. We are going to use it as an anchor or a home base. Put your hands on your belly and take a few breaths.*

Did you notice that your breath has two parts? The breath goes in and the breath goes out. Today we are going to focus on our breath.

But first, let's get set up to practice.

Consult your alphabetical roll list, and choose the first student to be the Mindfulness Helper for the day.

Invite today's Mindfulness Helper (MH) to come to the front of the class to sit next to you on a chair.

Say: *Let's all be happy for _____.* (sign language applause)

Prompt the MH to say slowly:

Let's get into our mindful bodies. **Pause**

Let's close our eyes or look down. **Pause**

Let's take three deep breaths. **Pause**

2. **Lead the class through a new practice: Count Ten Breaths**

    Say: *Let your breath settle back into its natural rhythm. You don't have to change it at all.*

    While you are breathing, place your hand on your belly and feel the little movement that happens when your breath goes in and out.

    Now move your hand to your chest and see what you feel there when your breath goes in and out. Notice where you felt your breath the most and keep your hand there, either on your belly or your chest.

    Now we're going to count ten breaths. You can count them any way you want to. You can count one in-breath, or inhale, and one out-breath, or exhale, as one whole breath. Or you can count each inhale and exhale as one breath. It doesn't matter how you count them. Try to keep your mind focused on counting your breaths.

    As soon as you notice that your mind has wandered away, try to bring it back to your counting, starting again at one. Try not to count higher than ten. Once you get to ten, start over at one or you can count backward.

Okay, let's try it. Remember, this is just for fun. Don't worry if your mind wanders. Just try to bring it back when you notice it has wandered. Let's start now.

You can give them a minute or more to try this, whatever seems appropriate.

Okay, now you can stop focusing on your counting, and let your mind be free to think or not think, whatever your mind wants to do.

Wait about 15 seconds.

Now let's take one more deep breath in and out. In a moment you will hear the sound of the bell and that will mean that it is time to open your eyes or look up.

Ask the MH to ring the bell when the mindful breathing is complete.

Ask the MH to return to their seat.

3. **Share**

    Ask:

    - What was that like for you?
    - Was it hard to keep your mind focused on your breath?
    - Did counting help you to focus?

    Remind the students: *It's perfectly normal for our minds to wander. This happens to all of us. With practices like this one, you are developing your ability to bring your focus back to what you need to be focusing on, even when it's not always super exciting. You're building a really important skill.*

    Try to practice this a couple of times this week and see if it gets any easier.

Kindness Pals

Invite students to share what they did for their previous pals over the last week.

Assign new Kindness Pals after they are finished sharing.

Kindness Pal Activity: My Kindness Pal's Favorite Things

Pass out one copy of the worksheet to each pair and ask them to sit together facing each other.

Go over the questions on the worksheet and make sure everyone understands the questions.

Say: *When I say go, you are going to start to interview each other. You can take turns asking each other questions and then go on to the next question.*

Sometimes people get stuck on thinking of a favorite thing. If you don't have a favorite book or movie or food just name one that you really like.

Also try to share the "Whys." Why do you like spaghetti? Why is Peace of Mind Class your favorite part of the school day? ;) Try to listen really carefully to your partner's answers.

When we are finished with the interviews I'm going to ask you to share some of what you learned about your Kindness Pal.

Okay, let's get started.

This might take 15-20 minutes although some kids will be done quickly. If kids are done too quickly, you might ask them to think of some bonus questions, offer some additional questions yourself, or ask them to go more into the "whys."

Share: Go through each question on the sheet and ask for some students to share what they learned about their Kindness Pal.

Ask: *Was anybody surprised about what they learned about their Pal? Did you find out that you had things in common that were unexpected?*

Closing words: *Our time is up for today. Thank you for a great class, everyone.*

Let's have a nice quiet moment for the bell. If you want to, you can close your eyes, picture your new Kindness Pal, and imagine yourself doing something kind for him or her this week.

Ring the bell.

Week 10
Thought Catcher

MINDFULNESS PRACTICE: Mindful Movement

OBJECTIVES: Notice when your mind wanders

Practice kindness

PREPARE: A bell or chime

Review the rules of the "Thought Catcher" Game

Your Kindness Pals list

Optional: Talking Object

This lesson continues our exploration of metacognition. This week's mindfulness practice is a game called Thought Catcher. This practice helps the children start to notice their thoughts and to make choices about which thoughts they want to focus on and which ones they'd like to let go. This is helpful in focusing attention where we need to focus it and also in increasing awareness of our thoughts in different situations.

This would be a good time to remind students that participation in the mindfulness practice itself is always optional. Mindfulness is a practice that is meant to help them, and it is wholly for their own use and benefit. Remind students that if they ever feel uncomfortable or anxious during a practice, they may choose to do another practice such as Take Five Breathing or, with your permission, to mindfully walk across the back of the room, for example, as long as their choice does not disturb others.

Mindfulness Practice

1. **Warm Up**

    Say: *Let's start out by doing some of our own whole-body Mindful Movements again. We can do some of the movements you created in previous lessons or we can make up new ones. Who wants to go first?*

    Do 3-5 of these movements with the class.

2. Introduce the Thought Catcher Game

Say: *Today we are going to be paying attention to our breath in a different way and we are going to be noticing what happens in our minds when we try to focus.*

Ask: *When I ask you to close your eyes and focus your mind on a sound or on your breath, what happens in your mind?*

Stop and let them share.

Say: *Yes, one thing we all notice is that our minds wander. The good news is that this is perfectly normal. It happens to everyone. And it's not usually a problem.*

But what happens when you are in math class and your teacher is telling you what the homework is and you are thinking about something else — like what you are having for dinner? That's not a great feeling.

In Mindfulness, we are trying to notice that moment when our minds wander and see where our minds go. Then we can decide if we want to redirect our minds. That's part of the fun. Paying attention to what is happening in our minds is called Metacognition. It just means thinking about thinking.

Describe the game like this:

I'm going to ask you to close your eyes and focus on counting your breath just the way we did in the last lesson. Once we start counting our breaths, I want you to try to notice what is happening in your mind.

You might notice that you are counting your breaths the whole time. That's fine. You might notice that as soon as you start counting your breaths you start thinking about lunch, or video games, or unicorns. That's fine too!

As soon as you notice that your mind has wandered, that a thought or a feeling has come into your mind, just point your finger.

Then see if you can bring your mind back to focusing on counting your breaths. Keep doing this until I ask you to stop. Let's try it.

3. **Introduce Mindfulness Helper**

    Invite today's Mindfulness Helper (MH) to come to the front of the class to sit next to you on a chair.

    Say: *Let's all be happy for* _____. *(sign language applause)*

    Prompt the MH to say: "Let's get into our mindful bodies. Let's close our eyes or look down. Let's take three deep breaths."

4. **Play "Thought Catcher"**

    Say: *Now let your breath settle back into its natural rhythm. Just breathe. Put your hand on your belly to help you to focus on your breath.*

    When you are ready, start to count your breaths. Every time you notice that your mind has wandered away from your breath, when a thought has popped into your mind, just point your finger and try to gently bring your mind back to your breath. You might have to do this over and over. That's perfectly fine.

    Wait about a minute or so and then say: *Now you can just let your mind be free to think or not think.*

    After a moment say: *Now let's take a nice deep breath and listen for the sound of the bell. When you hear the bell it will be time to open your eyes or look up.*

    Ask the MH to ring the bell when the "Thought Catcher" exercise is complete.

    Ask the MH to return to their seat.

5. **Share**

    After the game is over ask:

    - Did you notice that you were pointing your finger a lot today?
    - What did it feel like to pay attention to those thoughts as they came in?
    - What kinds of thoughts did you notice today?

Kindness Pals

Invite students to share what they did for their previous pals over the last week.

Assign new Kindness Pals after they are finished sharing.

 Kindness Pal Activity: Nine Words

Say: *Today you and your new Kindness Pals will have a challenge. You're going to try to come up with nine words that start with the first letter of each one of your names. You need to think of three foods, three animals, and three of anything at all. For example, if my name is Linda and your name is Jeremiah, then we have to think of three foods that start with L and three foods that start with J, three animals that start with L and three animals that start with J, and then three of anything that start with L and with J.*

L: Linguine, Lollipops, Lettuce

J: Jam, Jelly, Jellybeans

L: Lion, Lemur, Leopard

J: Jaguar, Jackal, Jellyfish

L: Lizard, Leotard, Lipstick

J: Jasmine, Jazz, Jump

After 5-10 minutes, give them a chance to share some of their answers with the class.

Closing words: *Okay our time is up for today. Thank you for a great class, everyone.*

Let's have a nice quiet moment for the bell. If you want to, you can close your eyes, picture your new Kindness Pal, and imagine yourself doing something kind for them this week.

Ring the bell.

Week 11
Time Traveling

MINDFULNESS PRACTICE: Past, Present, or Future

OBJECTIVES: Notice if your thoughts are mostly about the past, the future, or the present.

Practice kindness.

PREPARE: A bell or chime

Your Kindness Pals list

Optional: Talking Object

The object of this lesson is to help students develop the skills to keep their thoughts focused on the present. Students learn that they can choose to direct their thoughts away from worries about the past or future and focus their attention on what's happening right now.

You might like to reinforce the concept that having thoughts is normal, and that we are not asking them NOT to have thoughts. Instead, we are practicing the difficult skill of noticing our thoughts and then choosing to let them go if we want to.

When we recognize our thoughts, we have the opportunity to control our thoughts rather than allowing them to control us. This practice gives kids a way to notice what story they are telling themselves about future or past events, and to reflect on whether what they believe is actually true. We use the metaphor of a remote control and ask kids to consider who is pushing their buttons.

Mindfulness Practice

1. **Introduce Past, Present, or Future Thoughts**

   You might say: *The last time we met we practiced noticing our thoughts. We pointed our fingers every time a thought came into our minds.*

   Today we are going to be trying to notice if our thoughts are about the past, the present, or the future. Sometimes we are time traveling in our minds and we don't even realize it!

If I am thinking about my basketball game tomorrow my thoughts are in the…. (**future**).

If I am thinking about an argument I had with my little brother last night, my thoughts are in the…. (**past**).

If you are focusing on listening to me right now, your thoughts are in the…. (**present**).

Add hand gestures, saying: *We're going to add some hand gestures to help us with this. When we notice a thought that is about the past we'll point behind us. When we notice a thought that is about the future we'll point in front of us. When we notice a thought about the present we'll point down to the floor. Let's practice that a few times:*

If I am thinking about what I'm going to have for dinner… (point in front of you)

If I am thinking about what I had for dinner last night… (point behind you)

If I am thinking that I need to go to the bathroom…. (point down to the floor)

What if I suddenly start thinking about unicorns, or wondering whether narwhals like swimming? Do those thoughts fit into these three categories? Not really. So if we notice a thought like that let's make up a gesture for that.

Take their suggestions. It could be a shoulder shrug "I don't know" kind of gesture, or you could draw a question mark in the air….

Try it: *So today, after we get set up by the Mindfulness Helper, we are going to try to count our breaths. Only this time, every time you notice that your mind has wandered (and you know it will!) I want you to try to notice if it is a thought about the past, the present, or the future or something else. You'll use the hand gestures we created to help you stay focused.*

Once you've labeled each thought, see if you can bring your mind back to counting your breaths.

You might want to demonstrate this for them.

2. Mindfulness Helper

Invite today's Mindfulness Helper (MH) to come to the front of the class and sit next to you on a chair.

Say: *Let's all be happy for _____.* (sign language applause)

Prompt the MH to say: "Let's get into our mindful bodies. Let's close our eyes or look down. Let's take three deep breaths."

3. Lead the class through Past-Present-Future as described above.

Ask the MH to ring the bell when the Gravity Hands Practice is complete.

Ask the MH to return to their seat.

4. Share

After the mindfulness practice is complete say:

- Raise your hand if most of your thoughts were about the past.
- Raise your hand if most of your thoughts were in the present.
- Raise your hand if most of your thoughts were in the future.
- Raise your hand if you had a mixture.
- Raise your hand if you had some thoughts that didn't fit into those three categories.

Activity: Make an Anchor Chart

On a piece of chart paper make four columns labeled Past, Present, Future and "?".

Ask some of the children to share one of the thoughts they noticed and then let other children decide which column it should go into. Notice with the class that this isn't always easy and there can be more than one right answer. Notice any similarities and differences.

Reflect and Discuss

What's the point? It's important to help students connect this practice with ways it could be helpful to them.

To launch a discussion, you might ask:

- Why do you think it might be good to keep your mind focused on the present, on this moment?
- If your mind is always focused on what has already happened, or what hasn't happened yet, or what might never happen, what do you think you might be missing?

Discussion Points:

- When we try to notice where our thoughts are going, we can try to redirect them to where we want them to be. If you tend to worry a lot, your thoughts are mostly in the…. (future).
- Worrying doesn't help make things better and it doesn't stop bad things from happening. But it does keep you from enjoying the good stuff.
- If you notice that your thoughts are often in the future, see if you can try to focus your mind on something right here in the present moment. Try to notice what is good in this moment.
- Why do you think it might be a problem if your thoughts are mostly about things that have already happened? Sometimes we spend a lot of time ruminating about things that already happened even though we know that we can't change the past. Sometimes it can be good to redirect our thoughts to what is happening right now.

Kindness Pals

Invite students to share what they did for their previous pals over the last week.

Assign new Kindness Pals after they are finished sharing.

 Kindness Pal Activity: Nine Words

Say: Let's try the Nine Words Challenge again with your new Kindness Pal. *Today you and your new Kindness Pals will have a challenge. You're going to try to come up with nine words that start with the first letter of each one of your names. Last time we did Foods, Animals, and a free-for-all category. Let's keep the last one and think of two new categories.*

Take their answers and play the game as in Week 9.

After 5-10 minutes, give them a chance to share some of their answers with the class.

Closing words: *Okay our time is up for today. Thank you for a great class, everyone.*

Let's have a nice quiet moment for the bell. If you want to, you can close your eyes, picture your new Kindness Pal, and imagine yourself doing something kind for them this week.

Ring the bell.

Week 12
Keeping Your Focus

MINDFULNESS PRACTICE: Gravity Hands

OBJECTIVES: Practice keeping your focus when surrounded by annoying sounds.

Practice kindness.

PREPARE: A bell or chime

Gather noisemakers, such as scissors, a wind-up toy, a jar of pencils, a squeaky chair, etc. Use whatever you have around

A feather or another object to drop

Your Kindness Pals list

Optional: Talking Object

This is our final lesson of our Metacognition Unit. In this lesson, we'll be asking students to see how well they are able to put their skills to work to keep their attention focused where they want it to be, even through challenging distractions. This lesson can be quite fun for everyone! It also gives children a chance to experience what they are capable of. You might consider playing this game in future classes to allow children to see if their focusing skills are getting stronger. We'll begin with a new mindfulness practice called Gravity Hands.

Mindfulness Practice

1. **Introduce Gravity Hands**

   Gravity Hands is a very simple practice of slowly moving your hands up when you breathe in and then slowly lowering them down when you breathe out. It's fun to think about gravity while doing this practice. Making your inhale and exhale the same length can be very soothing and calming.

   Say: *Today we're going to learn another way of doing mindful breathing called Gravity Hands! Start out by stretching your arms straight out in front of you with your palms facing down. Hold them there and I'm going to count 30 seconds.* **Wait 30 seconds.**

Ask: *So what are you noticing? Are your arms starting to feel heavy, do you want to put them down? Is it getting harder? Let's put our arms down now.*

Ask: *Does anybody know why our arms started to feel heavy or it was hard to hold them up?*

Yes, it's because of gravity! Gravity is a force that pulls things down toward the earth. It's the reason that we aren't floating around the classroom right now! When we throw a ball up in the air what happens to it? That's right, it falls back down.

You can have kids demonstrate gravity by jumping up and noticing that they come right back down or dropping a feather and watching it fall.

Say: *Gravity is why it was hard to keep our arms outstretched — gravity wanted them to come down. Let's try it again.*

Repeat the arm activity from above reminding them to notice the pull of gravity.

Say: *Today we're going to do a mindful breathing practice called Gravity Hands. We're going to slowly bring our hands up, palms up, and then we're going to turn them over and slowly bring them down, palms down. Let's try that a few times.*

Now we're going to add breathing to it. When we slowly bring our hands up, we're going to breathe in slowly and gently. When we lower our hands back down, we're going to breathe out slowly and gently.

Let's try it for our Mindful Moment!

2. Mindfulness Helper

Invite today's Mindfulness Helper (MH) to come to the front of the class to sit next to you on a chair (or next to you on the floor).

Say: *Let's all be happy for _____.* (sign language applause)

Prompt the MH to say: "Let's get into our mindful bodies. Let's close our eyes or look down. Let's do Gravity Hands."

You or the Mindfulness Helper can lead the class through the practice again.

Ask the MH to ring the bell when the mindful breathing is complete.

Ask the MH to stay up front because they will be leading the second practice today.

Metacognition Practice

You might say:

Today I am going to challenge you. After the Mindfulness Helper gets us set up again, I am going to ask you to focus your mind on counting your breaths. We are going to try to notice any thoughts that pop into our minds like we did last time. We'll use the same hand gestures that we created last time. Let's review those.

Ask the students to demonstrate the Past, Present, Future, and "?" gestures you created during the last lesson.

Say: *So you are going to do that Time Traveling game again. But this time while you are doing that I'm going to be really annoying.*

I'm going to be making some sounds and trying to distract you. Your job is to keep your eyes closed or looking down, even if you are really curious, and keep your mind focused on counting your breaths and noticing your thoughts.

Anytime you get distracted you can go back and start counting at one. I will show you everything I used to make the sounds when we are done so don't be tempted to peek. Ready?

Prompt the MH to say: "Let's get into our mindful bodies. Let's close our eyes. Let's take three Gravity Hands breaths."

Say: *Now I'd like you to try to start counting your breaths as you breathe normally. As I said before I am going to try to distract you. I might make noises or do other things to take your focus off of your breath. Try really hard to keep your focus on counting your breaths, and don't open your eyes to peek. We'll share what happened when we are finished.*

Distract the class. After the children are set up and have begun their mindful breathing practice, you are going to try to distract them by being really annoying.

Walk around the room and make random noises. You might even tap someone on the top of the head or whisper someone's name.

Keep these distractions funny and silly so that the kids will feel safe and won't be scared.

Their job is to keep their eyes closed and try to keep focusing on counting their breaths.

Say: *Now take a deep breath, and listen for the sound of the bell. When you hear that sound it will be time to open your eyes.*

Ask the MH to ring the bell and return to their seat.

Reflect and Discuss

After the exercise, **ask**:

- Can you guess what I was using to make the sounds?
- What did you hear?
- Was it hard or easy to keep your focus?

Kindness Pals

Invite students to share what they did for their previous pals over the last week.

Assign new Kindness Pals after they are finished sharing.

 Kindness Pal Activity: Mirror Game

Say: *Now we're going to play a game with our new Kindness Pal. We are going to be moving mindfully and really focusing on what our Kindness Pal is doing. What do you think it means to move mindfully?*

Let some children share.

Say: *We're going to play a Mirror Game. You are going to take turns being the leader and doing slow movements with your body. Your Kindness Pal will try to be your reflection in the mirror and do the exact same movements. After one* *minute, I will ask you to switch and the other person will be the leader.* (You can demonstrate with a student so that they get the idea.)

Instruct the children to stand up facing their new Kindness Pal. Ask them to be mindful of other people's bodies when they choose their space. Use this as an opportunity to model moving mindfully.

Ask the children to choose the first leader. When you say "Go," the leader starts doing slow movements and the other person tries to follow those movements. Give them a minute or more and then say "Switch" and have them switch roles.

Encourage the children to focus on what their bodies feel like when they are moving.

You might say: *Notice how heavy your arms feel when you hold them out in front of you.*

When you are finished you can ask the students to share what it felt like to play the game. What was easy? What was hard about it?

Closing words: *Okay our time is up for today. Thank you for a great class, everyone.*

Let's have a nice quiet moment for the bell. If you want to, you can close your eyes, picture your new Kindness Pal, and imagine yourself doing something kind for them this week.

Ring the bell.

UNIT 4:
Feelings, Sensations, and Your Body

Week 13
Using Mindfulness to Take Care of Anger

MINDFULNESS PRACTICE: Gravity Hands and Blooming Breaths

OBJECTIVES: Act out a story to illustrate the concept of using mindful breathing to handle strong emotions.

Practice Gravity Hands.

Learn Blooming Breaths.

Practice kindness.

PREPARE: A bell or chime

Field Day Skit

Your Kindness Pal List

Optional: Talking Object

Welcome to our unit on Feelings, Sensations, and the Body. In this unit, we help children tune into the language of their bodies. When we are able to notice sensations in our bodies — perhaps a feeling of heat in the face, or tightness in the belly — we have an early indicator that a big emotion like anger is building up. Our physical sensations can give us the heads up we need to take care of our feelings and still be able to respond in the way that we want to in a challenging situation.

This would be a good time to remind students that participation in the mindfulness practice itself is always optional. Mindfulness is a practice that is meant to help them, and it is wholly for their own use and benefit. Remind students that if they ever feel uncomfortable or anxious during a practice, they may choose to do another practice such as Take Five Breathing or, with your permission, to mindfully walk across the back of the room, for example, as long as their choice does not disturb others.

Mindfulness Practice #1

Invite today's Mindfulness Helper (MH) to come to the front of the class to sit next to you on a chair.

Say: *Let's all be happy for _____. (sign language applause)*

Prompt the MH to say: "Let's get into our mindful bodies. Let's close our eyes or look down. Let's take three deep breaths with Gravity Hands."

Say: *In a moment you will hear the sound of the bell (or chime or whatever you are using). When you hear that sound, it will be time to open your eyes or look up.*

Ask the MH to ring the bell when the mindful breathing is complete and return to their seat.

Act it Out: The Field Day Skit

Say: *Today we are going to act out a story about some kids who get angry at school. Is getting angry at school harder than getting angry at home? What is different about it?*

Take a few answers.

Introduce the skit. Explain that this is a story about four kids who get mad at each other during a school activity. They will be demonstrating how people might feel differently when they get angry and how mindful breathing can help to calm you down when you are angry.

You will be the narrator and read the directions and dialogue aloud, and the kids will act out the directions and repeat the lines after you.

Choose students to represent the teacher, Mr. Gregal, and students Anas, Florence, Malek, and Imani.

Read the skit while student actors do the actions.

It was Field Day at Lafayette Elementary School, everybody's favorite day of the year. It was a whole day of being outside doing fun activities. Mr. Gregal's Small Potatoes were sure that they were going to be the only class who could do every single activity.

Mr. Gregal said, *"Okay class let's go out and have fun! Ready? Let's go!!"*

Anas, Florence, Malek, and Imani were on a team together. They were so excited!

First they went to the monkey bars station and they all climbed across really fast. *Students pantomime monkey bars.*

Then they went to the basketball toss station and they each made a basket. *Students take turns making baskets.*

Then they went to the dance station and they did really funny dances. *Students dance.*

Then they went to … *(let the kids make up some activities for them to act out)*

Everything was going great until they went to the water balloon toss. They were throwing water balloons to each other until suddenly…. POP!!! The water balloons burst and they all got soaked. *Students mime getting soaked.*

Everybody got mad, except for Malek.

Anas was mad. He felt like his face was getting hot and his hands clenched up into little fists. He said, *"Hey Florence! You got me all wet! You should have thrown the balloon more softly!"*

Florence was mad too. She was soaking wet and now Anas was yelling at her. She felt like crying and punching something. She said, *"Stop yelling at me! It wasn't my fault! You're being mean! I'm all wet too!"*

Imani was mad too. When she got mad she got really quiet. She just stood there and stared at Malek.

Malek said, *"Imani, are you okay? You look kind of mad."*

Imani said, *"I'm fine!"* But she didn't look fine. She looked stiff and still and tense.

Malek was the only one who wasn't mad. He thought it was funny to be all wet. He said, *"Come on you guys! It's just water! We're not made of sugar. Let's keep playing."*

Everybody said, *"No!"*

Malek said, *"Hey guys, if we don't calm down we're not going to finish all of the activities. Why don't we do some Gravity Hands. Mindful breathing can help us calm down when we're feeling angry, right?"* He started breathing in and out and raising his hands slowly up and down with his breath.

Anas didn't really feel like doing it but he really wanted to get to the other activities, especially the big relay race, so he joined Malek in doing Gravity Hands.

Imani and Florence decided to join in too. After a few minutes they were starting to feel better.

Anas said, *"Hey Florence, I'm sorry I yelled at you. Let's go to the big race. Last one there is a rotten egg!"* and he ran off.

Florence said, *"I'll beat you to it!"* and she ran off.

Imani said, *"What the heck is a rotten egg?"* Malek said, *"Who knows?! Let's go!"*

And they both ran off to the big relay race.

The End.

Reflect and Discuss

To launch a discussion, you might ask:

- Why were the kids angry?
- How did Anas feel when he was angry? What did he feel in his body?
- How did Florence feel? Was it the same as Anas?
- How did Imani feel when she was angry? Did she yell like Anas and Florence?
- Did mindful breathing help the kids calm down?
- What would have happened if they hadn't done Gravity Hands?
- Do you ever feel like you're not allowed to be angry at school?

Say:

It might seem like anger isn't allowed in school, but it is important to remember that all of our feelings are always allowed. But sometimes we are not in a place where we can express them the way we might want to. Like at school. This is why our mindful breathing can be so helpful.

Mindfulness Practice #2

This could be a good time to focus on the value of mindfulenss to us in these intense moments. We've included another practice you can introduce at this point if it feels helpful to your class.

Blooming Breaths is a nice way to help children calm themselves down when they are upset or need a break. The Blooming Breaths practice was created by one of my students. She had a little pond in her backyard that had water lilies floating in it. She loved the water lilies and the way that they opened up in the mornings and closed up in the evenings. It's fun to give kids lots of different ways to do mindful breathing. Adding a gesture helps to remind them of the practice and make it a little more tangible and easier to focus.

Introduce Blooming Breaths

Say: *Today we're going to learn a breathing practice called Blooming Breaths. Have you ever seen water lilies? They are those pretty white flowers that float on ponds. Water lilies are interesting because they open every morning and close up again every night. The flowers last for a few days.*

Let's pretend that our hands are like those water lilies. Hold your hands out in front of you with your palms up and then bring your fingers and thumb together. Then open your hands up and spread your fingers and thumb out wide. Slowly open and close your hands imagining that they are like the water lilies. Now let's add some breathing to it. Start with your "water lilies" closed. Then slowly and gently breathe in and open your lilies wide (stretch your fingers). Then slowly and gently breathe out and close your lilies up (fingers and thumbs together). Let's try that a few times slowly together.

Breathing, moving our hands, and thinking about water lilies can be a great way to help us to settle down when we are angry or nervous or having another kind of big emotion. Let's try it now!

Give students a chance to try it on their own.

Kindness Pals

Invite students to share what they did for their previous pals over the last week.

Assign new Kindness Pals after they are finished sharing.

Kindness Pal Activity: Mirror Game

Say: *Today we're going to play the Mirror Game again with our new Kindness Pal. We are going to be moving mindfully and really focusing on what our Kindness Pal is doing. You are going to take turns being the leader and doing slow movements with your body. Your Kindness Pal will try to be your reflection in the mirror and do the exact same movements. After one minute I will ask you to switch and the other person will be the leader.* You can demonstrate with a student so that they get the idea.

Instruct the children to stand up facing their new Kindness Pal. Ask them to be mindful of other people's bodies when they choose their space. Use this as an opportunity to model moving mindfully.

Ask the children to choose the first leader. When you say "Go," the leader starts doing slow movements and the other person tries to follow those movements. Give them a minute or more and then say "Switch" and have them switch roles.

Encourage the children to focus on what their bodies feel like when they are moving.

You might say: *Notice how heavy your arms feel when you hold them out in front of you.*

When you are finished you can ask the students to share what it felt like to play the game. What was easy? What was hard about it?

Closing words: *Okay our time is up for today. Thank you for a great class, everyone.*

Let's have a nice quiet moment for the bell. If you want to, you can close your eyes, picture your new Kindness Pal, and imagine yourself doing something kind for them this week.

Ring the bell.

Week 14
Body Scan

MINDFULNESS PRACTICE: Flashlight Body Scan

OBJECTIVES: Learn that we can be aware of what is happening in our bodies and begin to relate physical feelings to our emotions.

Practice kindness.

PREPARE: A bell or chime

Your Kindness Pals list

Optional: Talking Object

This lesson introduces a method of body scanning that you can use over and over again. It helps the children tune into what is happening in their bodies and their feelings.

This is a good time to remind your students that they always have a choice about whether to participate in a given mindfulness practice. We hope they will try, but it is always up to them. If you notice a child who is looking uncomfortable, remind them quietly that they have a choice about whether to participate. Offer them some alternatives that will not disturb others, such as choosing another practice, walking quietly at the back of the room if they really need to move, or just sitting quietly and thinking about something else until the practice is done. Try not to give them the option of doing something else like reading. Most kids will get something out of the practice just by sitting and being part of the group experience. Sitting quietly for a few minutes doing nothing can be a very healthy break for some kids.

As with any lesson in this curriculum, you can use this script to begin and then adapt it to make it your own in the future.

Mindfulness Practice

1. Introduce the practice of Body Scanning

Say: *Today we are going to learn a type of body scanning called "Flashlight Scanning." In a few minutes we are going to ask our Mindfulness Helper to get* us set up for Mindfulness practice. After we take our three deep breaths, I will guide you through the flashlight body scan.

Say: Let's start with this: Put your arms out in front of you with your palms facing each other. Clap your hands together hard and leave your hands about a foot apart. You will notice an intense tingling feeling.

Now, I want you to close your eyes, or look down into your lap if you don't feel comfortable closing your eyes, and put your arms out in front of you like I did. When I say "Go," we are all going to clap our hands. Make sure that you don't talk, but just quietly notice what you feel. Go.

Give them a moment to notice the feelings.

Say: Open your eyes or look up when you can't feel that tingling anymore.

Ask: What did that feel like? **Take a few answers.**

2. Mindfulness Helper

Invite today's Mindfulness Helper (MH) to come to the front of the class to sit next to you on a chair.

Say: Let's all be happy for _____. (sign language applause)

Prompt the MH to say: "Let's get into our mindful bodies. Close your eyes or look down into your lap. Let's take three deep breaths."

3. Body Scan

Say: Today we are going to take a little trip around our bodies with our minds.

Take your time with this and talk softly. Remind your students that it's okay if they don't feel anything; the important thing is just to try.

Remind them that you will be asking them questions but that they will be answering the questions in their own minds silently and that we will share later.

Use this script:

Today we are going to do a Flashlight body scan. You can lie down if you feel comfortable doing that; otherwise you may sit in a chair.

Close your eyes and try to make your body so still that the only thing you can feel moving is your breath. Imagine that you have a big flashlight hanging over your body. Imagine that you can operate this flashlight with your mind. Turn it on. Turn it off. Turn it on again.

Move it so that it is shining on your feet. Move it so that it is shining on your head. We're going to use the flashlight to help us to focus on different parts of our bodies.

Start by shining the flashlight on your right foot. Notice if you can feel any sensations there. Is it warm…. cold…. itchy…. do you feel your sock? Does it feel soft or scratchy? Are your shoes tight or loose?

Now move your flashlight to your left foot. Do you notice any differences? Is it warmer or colder than your right foot? What do you notice?

Now move your flashlight up to your knees. What do you feel there? Can you feel the fabric of your pants or leggings? Can you feel the air on your knees?

Now move your flashlight to your right hand. Can you still feel the tingling feeling from the big clap or has that gone away? Does your hand feel cold or warm, dry or a little sweaty?

Now move your flashlight to your left hand. What is different over there? Is one hand warmer than the other? How does your left hand feel?

Now move your flashlight to your belly. There is always something going on in your belly so it's a good place to notice sensations. Maybe it's almost time for lunch and you can feel that your stomach is empty. Maybe you have just eaten lunch and you can feel your food digesting. Maybe you can feel your belly rising and falling with your breath. Try to notice that for a few breaths.

Now move your flashlight to your chest. Maybe you can feel your heart beating. Maybe you can feel your chest rising and falling as your lungs fill up with air and empty again. Try to notice that for a few breaths.

Now move your flashlight up to your face. Shine it on your right eye. What do you feel there? What does it feel like to have your eyelid closed? Move it to your other eye? Any differences?

Move your flashlight to your nose. Can you feel the air going in and out? Maybe you can't. Just try to notice it.

Move your flashlight to your mouth. Focus on your tongue. What does it feel like? Is it dry or wet? Is it itchy?

Move your flashlight to your teeth. Can you feel your teeth without touching them with your tongue? If you have braces you definitely know what your teeth feel like when your braces have been tightened. How do you know that you have teeth if you can't see them?

Move your flashlight to the top of your head. Can you feel your hair with your mind?

Now pull your flashlight back so that it is shining on your whole body. What do you notice? Maybe you are feeling really relaxed and could lie here all day. Maybe you are feeling antsy and can't wait to get up. Any way that you feel is fine. Just try to notice what it feels like.

After a few moments, say: *Now let's take one more deep breath in and out. Let's listen to the sound mindfully and open your eyes or look up when you can't hear it anymore.*

Ask the MH to ring the bell and return to their seat.

Reflect and Dicsuss

Use these questions to guide a discussion.

- What did it feel like to travel through your body?
- What did you notice?
- Are you used to paying attention to your body?
- Would it be helpful to pay more attention to your body?
- What about when you are playing a sport?
- What about when you are in school?

Kindness Pals

Invite students to share what they did for their previous pals over the last week.

Assign new Kindness Pals after they are finished sharing.

Kindness Pal Activity: Kindness Pal Challenge

Say: *I'm going to set a timer for 90 seconds. You're going to sit with your new Kindness Pal and try to find out how many things you two have in common. Remember to ask each other questions and keep track. When I ring the bell, we'll share what we found out about each other.*

You can let the time go longer than 90 seconds if the kids seem to be having a good time.

Share. Come back together as a group and ask them to share something that they learned about their Kindness Pals.

This exercise is a great way to practice Mindful Listening and help them to develop an interest in others.

Closing words: *Okay our time is up for today. Thank you for a great class, everyone. Let's have a nice quiet moment for the bell. If you want to, you can close your eyes, picture your new Kindness Pal, and imagine yourself doing something kind for them this week.*

Ring the bell.

Week 15
Tummy Breaths

MINDFULNESS PRACTICE: Take 5 Breathing

OBJECTIVES: Learn deep belly breathing to help manage strong emotions.

Practice kindness.

PREPARE: A bell or chime

Your Kindness Pals list

Small objects (such as socks) to put on our belly

Optional: Talking Object

In today's lesson we are going to practice using deep belly breathing to help manage strong emotions. This way of breathing feels awkward at first, but breathing in and out engaging the abdominal muscles and pulling the diaphragm down allows the lungs to fill up more fully. We'll be practicing by putting an object on the belly and practicing lifting it up and down with the breath. But we'll start with an old favorite, Take Five Breathing. Have fun with it!

Mindfulness Practice

Invite today's Mindfulness Helper (MH) to come to the front of the class to sit next to you on a chair.

Say: *Let's all be happy for _____.* (sign language applause)

Prompt the MH to say: "Let's get into our mindful bodies. Let's close our eyes or look down. Let's take five deep breaths."

Say: *Let's practice our Take Five Breathing. Trace your hand while you breathe in and out five times.*

Say: *Now take a deep breath and listen for the sound of the bell. When you hear that sound it will be time to open your eyes.*

Ask the MH to ring the bell and return to their seat.

Where do you feel it? Noticing and managing anger.

In this section, students will learn to use deep belly breathing to notice and help manage anger.

Say: *Today we are going to be talking about breathing again. Paying attention to our breathing is a great way to practice mindfulness because our breath is always with us. We can't forget it or leave it at home.*

Today we are going to try doing something called deep belly breathing.

Deep belly breathing is a great way to help you calm down when you are really mad, angry, sad, or nervous.

Raise your hand if you have ever been really mad or angry.

Ask: *What does anger feel like in your body?*

Take a few answers.

Ask: *What does your breath feel like when you are angry?*

Take a few answers.

Demonstrate deep belly breathing. You might use this script:

We have all felt angry before. Taking a few deep belly breaths can really help you feel like yourself again. When we do belly breathing or Tummy Breaths, we are using our stomach muscles — our abdominal muscles. We are stretching out our stomach muscles to make room for our lungs to fill up fully with air. It feels a little funny at first because it's not the way we are used to breathing. But it's pretty easy once you get the hang of it! First watch me.

Place your hands on your belly and take a deep breath in through your nose and expand your belly as you breathe in. Make it a little exaggerated so that they can see it. Exhale through your mouth and flatten your stomach. Do this a few times.

Ask:

What did you notice about the way I was breathing? Did you see how my belly got bigger when I breathed in and flatter when I breathed out?

It's like I have a little balloon in my belly. When I breathe in I am filling the balloon full of air. When I breathe out I am emptying the balloon.

Let's get into our Mindful Bodies and try it together. Put your hands on your belly and take a deep breath in through your nose and try to imagine that you are filling the little balloon inside your belly with air.

Now breathe out slowly and gently through your mouth and imagine that you are emptying the balloon. Try that several times slowly and gently.

See your belly move.

A great way to practice deep belly breathing is with a small object that can rest on a child's belly. You can use whatever you have around for this. One idea is small, flat river rocks about the size of silver dollars. You can use small stuffed animals if you have enough or bean bags. You want something heavy enough that the students are aware that there is something on their bellies but not so heavy that they have to work to lift it.

Say, *Now we are going to practice our deep belly breathing. One way to practice this is while lying down.*

Please give students a choice about lying down or sitting up. Some children might feel uncomfortable or vulnerable lying down.

Ask for a volunteer to demonstrate. Have the volunteer lie down on their back in front of the class. Place the **small object** on their belly just above their belly button. Ask them to take a deep breath in through their nose and try to lift the object. Now ask them to take a nice slow deep breath out through their mouth and slowly lower the object. It might take them a while to get the hang of it. Ask the rest of the class to breathe along with them.

Next, you will be asking the class to try it. You might use these directions:

Now, are you ready to try it? Remember that this is a Mindfulness activity so we are going to be very quiet and calm while we are doing this. I am going to wait for everyone to find a place to lie or sit down. Once I see that you are ready with your body very still and your eyes closed or looking up at the ceiling, I am going to come around and hand you a small stone to put on your belly. Once you have the stone you can start practicing your deep belly breathing.

If students are sitting, they can hold the object against their stomach and practice that way.

Go around and hand them the stones or other small objects to put on their bellies. This might take a while but it's a nice quiet moment, and the kids seem to enjoy lying down.

Once everyone has their object you can ask them to breathe in unison.

Let's all take some deep belly breaths together. In and out, in and out, slowly and gently.

When doing this exercise with something like river rocks, you may end by asking everyone to imagine what their rocks look like—color, shape, size. Then give them a chance to use their hands to feel the rock while keeping their eyes closed and to see what they can notice about the rock. They can rub it against their cheek and smell it too. Once they have spent some time mindfully touching the rock, they can sit up, open their eyes, and look at their rocks. Students usually really love this part.

Encourage the children to practice their deep belly breathing when they go to bed at night with one of their own stuffed animals.

Kindness Pals

Invite students to share what they did for their previous pals over the last week.

Assign new Kindness Pals after they are finished sharing.

 Kindness Pal Activity: Kindness Pal Challenge

Say: *I'm going to set a timer for 90 seconds. You're going to sit with your Kindness Pal and try to find out how many things you two have in common. Remember to ask each other questions and keep track. When I ring the bell, we'll share what we found out about each other.*

You can let the time go longer than 90 seconds if the kids seem to be having a good time.

Share. Come back together as a group and ask them to share something that they learned about their Kindness Pals. This exercise is a great way to practice Mindful Listening and help them to develop an interest in others.

Closing: *Okay our time is up for today. Thank you for a great class, everyone. Let's have a nice quiet moment for the bell. If you want to, you can close your eyes, picture your new Kindness Pal, and imagine yourself doing something kind for them this week.*

Ring the bell.

Week 16
Squeeze and Release

MINDFULNESS PRACTICE: Squeeze and Release

OBJECTIVES: Learn a practice to help relax the body.

Practice kindness.

PREPARE: A bell or chime

Your Kindness Pals list

Optional: Talking Object

So far in this unit we've focused on ways to notice physical sensations in our bodies and to use mindfulness to take care of big emotions before they overwhelm us. Today we'll explore a new body-centered practice called Squeeze and Release, a great practice to do when you are feeling angry or frustrated or any kind of big emotion that makes you feel tight and tense in your body. You exaggerate the feeling of tension in your body and then deliberately try to relax. We've noticed that for some kids it seems easier to try to relax this way. It's also a great way to learn to pay attention to the way that feelings show up in your body. We'll also do a fun movement game that challenges our brains.

Mindfulness Practice

1. **Introduce Squeeze and Release**

   Say: *Today we're going to learn a mindful breathing practice that can help when your body gets really tight and tense. Have you ever noticed how your body feels when you get angry or frustrated? Do you feel relaxed and loose in your body?*

NOTE FROM LINDA: *I sometimes will demonstrate this by making my body look really relaxed and then say, "Oh I'm so frustrated!" in a really mellow voice. Then I'll make my body look really tight and scrunched up and say, "Hey I'm so relaxed!" in a really tense, tight voice. They usually find it hilarious and it's a good way to help them begin to notice how they feel in their bodies when they are experiencing different emotions.*

It's important to remember and to remind the kids that emotions feel differently for different people. Not everybody feels tight and tense when they get angry. Any way that they feel is fine.

Say: *If you feel tight and tensed up in your body when you get angry you might try something called Squeeze and Release. We'll start with our hands. We're going to breathe in slowly and gently while we are squeezing our hands into little balls. You don't have to do it really hard, but just squeeze it a little. Then when you slowly and gently breathe out you'll try to relax your hands. Let's try it!*

Try a few repetitions. Then move to the shoulders — squeeze them up toward the ears and then gently let them drop down. Squeeze the face and release, the stomach muscles, the feet, the whole body, and so on.

Say: *Let's try it for our Mindful Moment!*

2. **Mindfulness Helper**

    Invite today's Mindfulness Helper (MH) to come to the front of the class to sit next to you on a chair (or next to you on the floor).

    Say: *Let's all be happy for _____. (sign language applause)*

    Prompt the MH to say: "Let's get into our mindful bodies. Let's close our eyes or look down. Let's do Squeeze and Release."

    You or the Mindfulness Helper can lead the class through the practice again.

    Ask the MH to ring the bell when the mindful breathing is complete and return to their seat.

Focusing Practice: Move with Walk, Stop, Wiggle, Sit

Here's how to play. There are many levels of this game.

Give directions to play Walk, Stop, Wiggle, Sit

- We're going to play the game without talking so that everyone can hear the directions.
- You won't get "out" if you make a mistake. Just keep trying.
- Make sure that you are not talking and that you are not touching anybody else.

For this first round,

- When I say Walk, you are going to walk.
- When I say Stop, you are going to stop.
- When I say Wiggle, you are going to wiggle.
- When I say Sit, you are going to sit down. Got it?

Level 1:

Walk = Walk

Stop = Stop

Wiggle = Wiggle

Sit = Sit

Try it a few times, changing the order and timing of the commands.

Level 2:

Say: *This time we're going to switch things up. When I say Walk you are going to Stop. When I say Stop you are going to Walk. When I say Wiggle you are still going to Wiggle. When I say Sit you are still going to Sit. Okay?*

Walk = Stop

Stop = Walk

Wiggle = Wiggle

Sit = Sit

Try it a few times, changing the order and timing of the commands.

Level 3:

Say: *Okay now I'm going to make it a little harder. This time when I say Walk you are going to Stop. When I say Stop you are going to Walk. When I say Wiggle you are going to Sit and when I saw Sit you are going to Wiggle.*

Walk = Stop

Stop = Walk

Wiggle = Sit

Sit = Wiggle

Try it a few times, changing the order and timing of the commands.

Note: You can make many more variations of this game — adding more levels, letting students lead the game, adding in different movements, etc. Have fun! Start out with a few levels and then add on more each time you play it. You'll be playing again in a couple of weeks.

Kindness Pals

Invite students to share what they did for their previous pals over the last week.

Assign new Kindness Pals after they are finished sharing.

 Kindness Pal Activity: Kindness Pal Challenge

Say: *I'm going to set a timer for 90 seconds. You're going to sit with your Kindness Pal and try to find out how many things you two have in common. Remember to ask each other questions and keep track. When I ring the bell, we'll share what we found out about each other.*

You can let the time go longer than 90 seconds if the kids seem to be having a good time.

Share. Come back together as a group and ask them to share something that they learned about their Kindness Pals. This exercise is a great way to practice Mindful Listening and help them to develop an interest in others.

Closing: *Okay our time is up for today. Thank you for a great class, everyone. Let's have a nice quiet moment for the bell. If you want to, you can close your eyes, picture your new Kindness Pal, and imagine yourself doing something kind for them this week.*

Ring the bell.

Week 17
Mindful Eating

MINDFULNESS PRACTICE: Mindful Eating

OBJECTIVES: Apply our mindfulness skills to our everyday lives.

Practice kindness.

PREPARE: A bell or chime

Enough raisins for all of your class to have one or two

Your Kindness Pals list

Optional: Talking Object

This week we'll continue our focus on feelings and sensations through the practice of Mindful Eating. Kids usually really enjoy this slow way to investigate a raisin — what does it smell like, taste like, look like, feel like in your mouth, sound like when you chew, and so on. If a child does not want to put the raisin in their mouth, that's fine! We will be exploring it in many ways. We hope this practice will inspire your students to try eating mindfully at home too. Have fun!

Mindfulness Practice

Invite today's Mindfulness Helper (MH) to come to the front of the class to sit next to you on a chair.

Say: *Let's all be happy for _____. (sign language applause)*

Prompt the MH to say: "Let's get into our mindful bodies. Let's close our eyes. Let's take five deep breaths."

Say: *Let's practice our Take Five Breathing. Trace your hand while you breathe in and out five times.*

Say: *Now take a deep breath, and listen for the sound of the bell. When you hear that sound it will be time to open your eyes.*

Ask the MH to ring the bell and return to their seat.

Practice Noticing Sensations: Mindful Eating

To introduce our Mindful Eating activity, you might say:

Now we are going to see what it feels like to eat something mindfully.

I am going to give you each one raisin. I'd like you to put your hand out in front of you. Please wait for me to bring you your raisin.

When you get your raisin just let it sit there on your open hand, please don't touch it or move it until I ask you to.

If you think you don't like raisins, don't worry. We are going to do a lot of different things with the raisin and you don't have to eat it if you don't want to.

Place a raisin in each child's hand.

Now that everyone has their raisin, I'd like you to take a look at yours. Don't touch it. Just use your eyes and see what you notice about your raisin. Who would like to share what they see?

Take a few responses.

Now I'd like you to notice how your raisin smells. What do you notice? Try smelling your raisin with your eyes closed and then with your eyes open. Do you notice any difference?

Encourage the children not to get too focused on whether or not they like the raisin. Encourage them to notice the raisin without judgment.

Now let's bring our attention to how our raisin feels. Take your finger and gently touch your raisin. What do you notice?

Now this might sound funny, but I'd like you to notice what your raisin sounds like. Pick it up with your fingers and put it next to your ear. If you wiggle it back and forth a little with your fingers you might notice a sound. What do you notice?

Now listen very carefully to these instructions.

Place your raisin right in the middle of your tongue and keep your mouth open.

Raise your hand if you can taste your raisin.

Try moving the raisin with your fingers to different places on your tongue and notice if your raisin tastes different in different parts of your tongue.

Now very gently take a bite of your raisin. Notice what happens. Does your raisin taste different than it did before you bit into it? Now you can chew your raisin. Notice what it feels like when you swallow it. See how long you can feel it going down.

Reflect and Discuss

Use these questions to help the class reflect on their experience.

- What did it feel like to eat mindfully?
- Is this the way you usually eat?
- Can you imagine yourself eating your dinner mindfully tonight?

You might conclude with: *Your assignment today is to try to eat one thing mindfully today. Enjoy!*

Kindness Pals

Invite students to share what they did for their previous pals over the last week.

Assign new Kindness Pals after they are finished sharing.

 ### Kindness Pals Activity: Kindness Pal Challenge

Say: *Let's try the Nine Words Challenge again with your new Kindness Pal. Today you and your new Kindness Pals will have a challenge. You're going to try to come up with nine words that start with the first letter of each one of your names. Since we've been doing Mindful Eating let's think of nine foods that start with the first letter of each one of your names.*

Play the game as in Week 10.

After 5-10 minutes, give them a chance to share some of their answers with the class.

Closing words: *Okay, our time is up for today. Thank you for a great class, everyone. Let's have a nice quiet moment for the bell. If you want to, you can close your eyes, picture your new Kindness Pal, and imagine yourself doing something kind for them this week.*

Ring the bell.

UNIT 5:
Kindness and Compassion

Week 18
Kindness Chain

MINDFULNESS PRACTICE: Blooming Breaths

OBJECTIVES: Show the power of our words and illustrate how one act of kindness can set off a chain of kindness.

Practice kindness.

PREPARE: A bell or chime

Your Kindness Pals list

Optional: Talking Object

We warmly welcome you to Unit 5: Kindness and Compassion. Since the beginning of the year, your students have been practicing kindness weekly. Take a moment to reflect on how your classroom community has changed as a result. What have you noticed?

In this unit, we are going to focus on the power of our words to help or harm. In this lesson, we will introduce this concept and then create a Kindness Chain. We'll talk about the way one kind word or act may create a chain of kind words or acts, rippling out to others.

We hope you and your students continue to enjoy the Kindness Pal activities every week.

Mindfulness Practice

Today's mindfulness practice is Blooming Breaths, introduced in Week 13.

Invite today's Mindfulness Helper (MH) to come to the front of the class to sit next to you on a chair (or next to you on the floor).

Say: *Let's all be happy for _____. (sign language applause)*

Prompt the MH to say: "Let's get into our mindful bodies. Let's close our eyes or look down. Let's take three deep Blooming Breaths."

Ask the MH to ring the bell when the mindful breathing is complete.

Ask the MH to return to their seat.

Mindful Speaking Practice: The Power of Words

1. Write on the board: "Words are like toothpaste."

Say: *For the next few classes we are going to switch gears a bit and talk about how we treat other people. We're going to talk about how to treat others with compassion and kindness. Today we are going to be focusing on how we talk to other people.*

Ask the kids to comment on what they think "Words are like toothpaste" means.

You might say: *When I say "words are like toothpaste," I am thinking about how once you squeeze the toothpaste out of the tube, it is impossible to put it back in.*

The same is true for our words.

Once you say something to someone, it is out there. Even if you really regret it or didn't really mean it, it's still out there. There is no way to put the words back in your mouth and make them disappear. That is why it's so important to think about our words before we say them and to recognize that our words have power.

Words are so powerful that with our words we can make someone feel wonderful. For example, I might say to my friend, "Wow, you are such an amazing artist! You should enter a competition."

My friend might respond in a positive way, and my words might give her the confidence to enter that contest and continue to make her art.

But what might happen if I say to my friend, "Uh, that drawing doesn't look anything like a horse. Maybe you should stick to baseball." What do you think might happen?

Pause for some comments.

So maybe my friend will say "Well, that's your opinion, but I love drawing and I'm going to keep trying."

Or maybe my friend will feel embarrassed and awful and will crumple up her paper and never draw again.

Our words have a lot of power. So it's important to think about what we say. Over the next few lessons, we are going to be thinking about our words in a few different ways.

Today we are going to be using our words to make people feel good.

Today we are going to make a Kindness Chain.

Kindness Practice: The Kindness Chain

We are going to go around the circle, and I'd like you to say something kind about the person sitting to your right. For example, I might say, "Cheryl, you are an awesome friend."

Cheryl might say, "Thanks!" and then turn to the person on her right and say, "Harry, you are really good at building things."

And we'll go around the circle like that. Every once in a while when we play this game somebody's mind goes blank, and they can't think of anything to say. Even if they are sitting next to their best friend! If that happens to you, don't worry. Just say, "I need some help." I will choose a volunteer to say something kind about that person and then we'll continue going around the circle.

When we're done we'll go around the circle in the other direction.

This is a chance to use the power of our words to make people feel really good, so let's try hard to take it seriously and make sure that everybody feels good. Ready to start?

Reflect and Discuss

Ask the children to share what it felt like to give and receive these compliments and what it feels like to use the power of your words for good.

Kindness Pals

Invite students to share what they did for their previous pals over the last week.

Assign new Kindness Pals after they are finished sharing.

 Kindness Pals Activity: Kindness Pal Challenge

Say: *Today, instead of finding out how many things we have in common, we are going to be trying to find out how many ways we are different from our new Kindness Pal.*

Say: *I'm going to set a timer for 90 seconds. You're going to sit with your Kindness Pal and try to find lots of things that are different about you. Remember to ask each other questions and keep track. When I ring the bell, we'll share what we found out about each other.*

You can let the time go longer than 90 seconds if the kids seem to be having a good time.

Share. Come back together as a group and ask them to share something that they learned about their Kindness Pals.

Closing words: *Okay, our time is up for today. Thank you for a great class, everyone. Let's have a nice quiet moment for the bell. If you want to, you can close your eyes, picture your new Kindness Pal, and imagine yourself doing something kind for them this week.*

Ring the bell.

Week 19
Heartfulness

MINDFULNESS PRACTICE: Heartfulness

OBJECTIVES: Use the practice of thinking kind thoughts to increase feelings of compassion and empathy for yourself and others.

Practice kindness.

PREPARE: A bell or chime

Heartfulness Worksheet

Your Kindness Pals list

Optional: Talking Object

In the last lesson, students practice saying kind things about and to each other. In this lesson, we learn a compassion practice called Heartfulness that allows us to extend kindness and compassion to ourselves and also to others outside of our class and school. Heartfulness helps children strengthen their sense of compassion and empathy. It can also help them to let go of angry feelings they may have toward others.

Mindfulness Practice

Introduce Heartfuness. Say: *Today we are going to do something called Heartfulness. This just means that we are going to be thinking about a person and sending them kind thoughts.*

But we aren't going to be making them a card or talking to them. We are going to be sending them kind thoughts in our minds.

Invite today's Mindfulness Helper (MH) to come to the front of the class to sit next to you on a chair.

Say: *Let's all be happy for _____. (sign language applause)*

Prompt the MH to say: "Let's get into our mindful bodies. Let's close our eyes or look down. Let's take three deep breaths."

Say: *I'd like you to think about someone who makes you happy. Someone you see every day, at home or at school. It could be someone in your family, a friend, a teacher, even a pet. Just choose someone and try to picture them happy and smiling. Picture them doing something that makes them happy. … Try to notice how you feel when you think about this person.*

Now, if you'd like to, put your hand over your heart and repeat these words in your mind while you think about this person:

May you be happy. **Wait a moment.**

May you be healthy. **Wait a moment.**

May you be peaceful. **Wait a moment**.

Take a moment to notice how you feel. Any way that you feel is fine, even if you feel nothing. Just try to notice it.

This might feel a little strange, but this time we are going to send kind thoughts to ourselves. Imagine yourself happy and smiling, doing something that you like to do. Now repeat these words in your mind.

May I be happy. **Pause**.

May I be healthy. **Pause**.

May I be peaceful. **Pause**

Again, try to notice how you feel. Does it feel different to send kind thoughts to yourself? Any way that you feel is fine. Just try to notice it.

In a moment you will hear the sound of the bells and that will mean that it is time to open your eyes. So just get ready for that.

Ask the MH to ring the bell when the mindful breathing is complete and return to their seat.

Reflect and Discuss

Ask:

- What does it feel like to send kind thoughts to yourself?
- What does it feel like to send kind thoughts to others?

Say: *Sometimes practicing heartfulness can make us feel like being kinder to ourselves and to others.*

Discussion Points

- Many children are uncomfortable sending kind thoughts to themselves thinking it makes them selfish.
- You can talk about the importance of treating ourselves with kindness and how we are often sending ourselves unkind thoughts throughout the day without even noticing it.
- You can remind the students that they can use heartfulness when they feel sad.

As the children get comfortable with this practice, you can extend it. Here are three ideas:

- You may invite the children to send heartfulness to sick or absent classmates.
- You may also suggest they send heartfulness to someone they are mad at.
- Children are often very aware of people in their community or in the world who are suffering. This practice gives them a way to express compassion for people they don't know.

Activity: Heartfulness Worksheet

Hand out copies of the Heartfulness worksheet to students.

Invite students to draw a picture of a person they sent Heartfulness to. They will have a chance to share this drawing and talk about it with their Kindness Pals.

Kindness Pals

Invite students to share what they did for their previous pals over the last week.

Assign new Kindness Pals after they are finished sharing.

Kindess Pal Activity: Sharing

Sit with your new Kindness Pal and share your drawing and tell them about who you were sending your kind thoughts to.

Closing: *Okay our time is up for today. Thank you for a great class, everyone. Let's have a nice quiet moment for the bell. If you want to, you can close your eyes, picture your new Kindness Pal, and imagine yourself doing something kind for them this week.*

Ring the bell.

Week 20
Empathy

MINDFULNESS PRACTICE: Take Five Breathing, Four Square Breathing, or Gravity Hands

OBJECTIVES: Developing awareness of the feelings of others.

Practice kindness.

PREPARE: A bell or chime

Copies of the *"Should We Let Him Play?"* Skit found in Resource Section

Your Kindness Pals list

Optional: Talking Object

This week we will be focusing on developing our awareness of other people's feelings and making kind choices. We'll introduce personal choice in the mindfulness practices today, again reminding students that these practices are for them. We'll then act out a skit to focus on empathy and inclusion.

Mindfulness Practice

1. Warm-up

Say: *Let's start today by making up our own ways of doing mindful movements. We've done this before. Let's try to use our whole bodies and link our breathing to the movement.*

Invite the kids to create their own Mindful Movements and ask a few to share. Encourage everybody to try each idea.

2. Mindfulness Helper

Invite today's Mindfulness Helper (MH) to come to the front of the class to sit next to you on a chair (or next to you on the floor).

Say: *Let's all be happy for _____.* (sign language applause)

Say: *Today when the Mindfulness Helper asks us to take deep breaths, you can do Take Five Breathing, Four Square Breathing, or Gravity Hands, or you can create a new way to take deep breaths. Remember that whatever you do needs to be calm and quiet to go along with your calm, quiet, deep breaths.*

Prompt the MH to say: "Let's get into our mindful bodies. Let's close our eyes or look down. Let's take three deep breaths."

Say: *After you are done taking your deep breaths, let your breath settle back into its natural rhythm. Just breathe in and out normally. Put a hand on your tummy and see if you can make the rest of your body so still that the only thing that you feel moving is your breath.*

Wait about 30 seconds.

Say: *In a moment you will hear the sound of the bell. When you hear that sound, it will be time to open your eyes if they are closed.*

Ask the MH to ring the bell when the mindful breathing is complete and return to their seat.

Act it Out: Should We Let Him Play?

In this skit, "Should We Let Him Play," we explore empathy for others and the power of words to harm and help.

Ask: *Can anybody think of a time that somebody helped you when you were going through a hard time? Or a time when somebody stood up for you when somebody else wasn't being nice to you?*

Take some answers.

Say: *We have been practicing metacognition — the practice of thinking about and noticing your own thoughts. Today we're going to to try to imagine how other people might be feeling. That is called empathy. We'll be thinking about treating people the way that we would like to be treated.*

Today we are going to do a skit. This skit is about what happens when a new kid is being left out at school. Three other kids are talking about him. One child is trying to get them to include him by helping them see things from his perspective and relate to him. Once they can see things from his point of view, they decide to include him.

Read through the script one time going around the room taking turns reading lines.

Assign parts to 7 students. Feel free to change the names to suit your class.

Have your first cast act out the skit.

Re-assign parts and have your second cast act out the skit.

Reflect and Discuss

To launch a discussion, you might ask:

- Why were the kids excluding the new kid?
- What convinced them to ask him to join them?
- Have you ever been excluded? How did it feel? What were the circumstances?
- Have you ever excluded someone? Did you realize that you were doing it? Did you think about the feelings of the person being excluded?
- Why do you think kids are more likely to get bullied when they are being excluded?
- What did it feel like to play the different parts? The kid being excluded, the kids doing the excluding, the kid standing up for the new kid?

Kindness Pals

Invite students to share what they did for their previous pals over the last week.

Assign new Kindness Pals after they are finished sharing.

 Kindness Pals Activity: Kindness Pal Challenge

Talk with your Kindness Pal about a time that you felt like you were left out or even a time when you didn't include someone and later wished that you had.

Closing words: *Okay, our time is up for today. Thank you for a great class, everyone. Let's have a nice quiet moment for the bell. If you want to, you can close your eyes, picture your new Kindness Pal, and imagine yourself doing something kind for them this week.*

Ring the bell.

UNIT 6: Brain Science

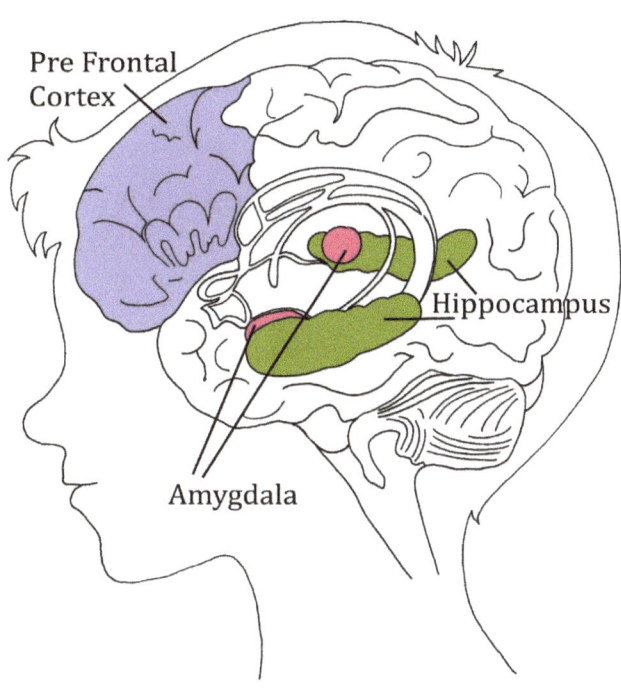

Week 21
Rosie's Brain

MINDFULNESS PRACTICE: Gravity Hands

OBJECTIVES: Learn about how three parts of our brain — the amygdala, hippocampus, and the prefrontal cortex — operate in regulating our emotions and reactions to stimuli.

Practice kindness.

PREPARE: A bell or chime

Rosie's Brain by Linda Ryden

Your Kindness Pals list

Optional: Brainy the Puppet

Optional: Talking Object

Video of Dr. Daniel Siegel's Hand Model of the Brain. Watch this before class. This video is for the teacher, not the students. http://www.drdansiegel.com/resources/everyday_mindsight_tools/

Diagram of the brain found in Resource Section

Our brains are complex and quite amazing parts of our bodies. In this curriculum, we offer a very simplified look at how our brains work in order to help children understand why we practice mindfulness and how it helps. We focus on two important components of the limbic system, the amygdala and the hippocampus, and also on the integrating portions of the brain's cortex, the prefrontal cortex.

To make these concepts accessible we'll be reading a book called *Rosie's Brain* by Linda Ryden. In this book, students will be introduced to three characters representing the amygdala, hippocampus, and prefrontal cortex.

We will start with Gravity Hands.

Mindfulness Practice

Invite today's Mindfulness Helper (MH) to come to the front of the class to sit next to you on a chair (or next to you on the floor).

Say: *Let's all be happy for _____.* (sign language applause)

Prompt the MH to say: "Let's get into our mindful bodies. Let's close our eyes or look down. Let's take three Gravity Hands breaths."

Say: *After you are done taking your deep breaths, let your breath settle back into its natural rhythm. Just breathe in and out normally. Put a hand on your tummy and see if you can make the rest of your body so still that the only thing that you feel moving is your breath.*

Wait about 30 seconds.

Say: *In a moment you will hear the sound of the bell. When you hear that sound, it will be time to open your eyes if they are closed.*

Ask the MH to ring the bell when the mindful breathing is complete and return to their seat.

Read and Discuss

Note: If your students have had the *Peace of Mind Core Curriculum for First and Second Grade* then they will have already been introduced to our book for today, *Rosie's Brain*. You can alter your introduction a little to remind them that they have heard this story before but that we will be revisiting it today.

Prepare to read *Rosie's Brain*.

Say: *Today we are going to start learning about our brains. Our brains are amazing and complicated and learning a little bit about how they work can be really helpful. We're going to start out by reading a story about a little girl named Rosie who gets really mad when she doesn't get what she wants.*

Read the story. Stopping along the way, ask these questions:

- Why was Rosie angry?
- What did her Amygdala (Amy) want her to do?
- Was Amy's idea (smashing the piano) a good one?
- How did her Hippocampus (Miss Pickles) help her?
- How did her PFC help her?
- Can you think of another way to solve Rosie's problem?

Kindness Pals

Invite students to share what they did for their pals over the last week.

Assign new Kindness Pals after they are finished sharing.

 Kindness Pal Activity: Kindness Pal Challenge

Say: *I'm going to set a timer for 90 seconds. You're going to sit with your Kindness Pal and try to find out how many things you two have in common. Remember to ask each other questions and keep track. When I ring the bell, we'll share what we found out about each other.*

You can let the time go longer than 90 seconds if the kids seem to be having a good time.

Share. Come back together as a group and ask them to share something that they learned about their Kindness Pals. This exercise is a great way to practice Mindful Listening and help them to develop an interest in others.

Closing words: *Okay, our time is up for today. Thank you for a great class, everyone. Let's have a nice quiet moment for the bell. If you want to, you can close your eyes, picture your new Kindness Pal, and imagine yourself doing something kind for them this week.*

Ring the bell.

Week 22
Helping Amy (Amygdala)

MINDFULNESS PRACTICE: Choice of Take Five Breathing, Gravity, Four Square Breathing

OBJECTIVES: Learn about how three parts of our brain — the amygdala, hippocampus and the prefrontal cortex — operate in regulating our emotions and reactions to stimuli.

Practice kindness.

PREPARE: A bell or chime

Video of Dr. Daniel Siegel's Hand Model of the Brain. Watch this before class. This video is for the teacher, not the students. http://www.drdansiegel.com/resources/everyday_mindsight_tools/

Diagram of the brain found in Resource Section

Your Kindness Pals list

Optional: Talking Object

We not only want children to develop mindfulness skills that will be helpful to them for life, we want them to understand why they help. Understanding how our amygdala functions can be liberating. Diving into the brain science helps kids understand why they feel big emotions like anger or fear. It helps them see that often big emotions are the result of our amygdala trying to protect us. It also clarifies that we all have these emotions, and that we can develop skills to manage big emotions — not to make them go away, but to choose how we respond to them.

If your students have previously had the *Peace of Mind Core Curriculum for First and Second Grades,* they may be familiar with this material. A review is always helpful!

Mindfulness Practice

Invite today's Mindfulness Helper (MH) to come to the front of the class to sit next to you on a chair (or next to you on the floor).

Say: *Let's all be happy for _____.* (sign language applause)

Say: *Today you'll get to choose what mindfulness practice you'd like to do. You can choose from Take Five Breathing, Four Square Breathing, and Gravity Hands. When the Mindfulness Helper says "Let's take three deep breaths" you can decide what you'd like to do.*

Prompt the MH to say: *"Let's get into our mindful bodies. Let's close our eyes or look down. Let's take three deep breaths."*

Say: *After you are done taking your deep breaths, let your breath settle back into its natural rhythm. Just breathe in and out normally. Put a hand on your tummy and see if you can make the rest of your body so still that the only thing that you feel moving is your breath.*

Wait about 30 seconds.

Say: *In a moment you will hear the sound of the bell. When you hear that sound, it will be time to open your eyes if they are closed.*

Ask the MH to ring the bell when the mindful breathing is complete and return to their seat.

Brain Science: The Hand Model of the Brain

Say: *Today we are going to be learning more about our brains.*

Hold up your hand in the shape of the hand model.

Can you do this with your hand? Tuck your thumb inside and then fold your fingers over your thumb. Now your hand looks a little bit like your brain.

Hold your hand up next to your head.

The first part is the amygdala. The amygdala is the little part of your brain inside here. Do you remember what the amygdala was called in Rosie's Brain? That's right — Amy!

Lift your fingers to show the tucked-in thumb.

The Amygdala

The amygdala (or Amy) is the part of your brain that reacts to things. This is the part of the human brain that developed first. Even cave people had amygdalas. What kinds of things were the cave people worried about? Were they worried about being late for school or getting all of their homework done? (They were worried about survival.)

Cave people were pretty much only worried about finding food and trying not to be somebody else's food. So their brains developed to help them with this.

If a cave man was walking through the forest and a saber-toothed tiger jumped out from behind a rock, what choices did he have? (Run away, fight, or freeze and hope the tiger doesn't see him.)

Those are the things that amygdalas do best. The amygdala helps us decide in a flash whether to run away, or try to fight the tiger, or to stay very still and hope the tiger doesn't see us. This is called the "fight, flight, or freeze reflex."

When the Amygdala Overreacts

The fight, flight, or freeze reflex was really helpful to our early ancestors and still helps to keep us safe today. But sometimes our amygdala can't tell the difference between real danger and something that you just don't like. It can overreact.

I'll bet we can all think of times when our amygdala was in charge (when it would have been better if it weren't). If your grown-up says you can't have ice cream after dinner, your amygdala says, "No!! That's not fair! I WANT ICE CREAM!"

If you are playing basketball and somebody comes up and takes your ball, your amygdala says, "Hey give it back!! It's mine!!" Your amygdala wants you to grab the ball back. You're not actually in danger when you don't get ice cream or someone takes the ball you're playing with. But your amygdala can react like you are.

Ask: *Can you think of a time when your amygdala told you to do or say something like that?*

Your amygdala feels scared sometimes too. Your amygdala might tell you not to jump off the diving board or not to raise your hand in class to answer a hard question. Your amygdala might tell you not to try out for the travel soccer team or for a solo in a concert. But is not getting the solo in the concert the same thing as getting eaten by a saber-toothed tiger? Nope. But your amygdala can't always tell the difference.

Ask: Can you think of a time when your amygdala was trying to protect you from something?

Your amygdala is wonderful and really wants to take care of you, to protect you. When it thinks you are in danger it takes over and it's almost like it turns off the other parts of the brain. We'll talk more about that next time. But if we only listened to our amygdala, we wouldn't be very happy. We'd be in fights with people all of the time, and we wouldn't do anything that we are scared to do, even really fun things like learning how to ride a bike or learning how to dive.

Sometimes our Amygdala needs a little help

So sometimes our amygdala is trying to help us. But sometimes it seems like our amygdala could use a little help. Can you think of something that we can do to help our amygdala? That's right! We can do mindful breathing. What are some of the mindful breathing practices that we've learned so far that could help us to take care of our amygdala? (Take Five Breathing, Gravity Hands, Four Square Breathing, etc.)

Act it Out: Ice Cream Drama and Crossing the Street

Today we are going to do a little role-playing and try to notice what it feels like when our amygdala is trying to help us and when our amygdala might need a little help.

Scenario 1: Ice Cream Drama

Choose two volunteers to be Student A and Student B (or give them names or use theirs):

Choose two kids to act out the story. Ask them to pantomime what you are describing in the story — if you say they are jumping up and down, the kids will jump up and down. You will be the narrator and you will read their lines and then the kids can repeat the lines after you read them.

Say: *Student A and Student B are eating ice cream cones while they walk down the street. Student A trips a little and bumps into Student B and knocks their ice cream cone onto the ground.*

Student B *looks at their ice cream on the ground and yells, "My ice cream! It's on the ground! I can't believe you did that!"*

Student A *looks shocked and says, "I didn't do it on purpose! You should have been more careful!"*

Ask the students to freeze.

Ask the class: *Why did Student B yell at Student A? Were they in danger? Did Student A do it on purpose? What was happening in Student B's brain?* (The amygdala took over and went into fight mode.)

Was "fight" a great way to deal with the problem? Did it get the ice cream back? Did it make Student A upset? Did it make things better? Was Student B's amygdala helping them or hurting them?

How could Student B help their amygdala? That's right — they could take some deep breaths. Let's see what happens.

Unfreeze the actors.

Student B *feels angry but takes a moment to take a few deep breaths. (Have Student B do Gravity Hands)*

Then Student B *says sadly, "Oh no! My ice cream! Ugh!"*

Student A *says, "Oh I'm so sorry! I didn't mean to knock it down.*

Student B *says, "I know, it was just an accident."*

Student A *says, "Maybe we can get you a new one. I have half the money. Do you have any money left?*

Student B *says, "Yeah I do. Thanks!!"*

Student A says, *"No problem." And they get a new ice cream cone for Student B.*

The End

Say: *Let's try another scenario.*

Scenario 2: Crossing the Street

Choose three volunteers to be Students A, B, and Student C.

Ask them to pantomime what you are describing in the story - if you say they are jumping up and down, the kids will jump up and down. You will be the narrator and you will read their lines and then the kids can repeat the lines after you read them.

Say: *Student A and Student B are walking home from school. They are about to cross the street. They look to the left and then they look to the right. Student A steps off of the curb into the street when Student B notices someone on a bike (Student C) coming toward them.*

Student B *says "Yikes!" and jumps back onto the curb and pulls Student A back too.*

Student A *says, "What was that?!" and then sees the bike go by.*

Student B *says, "Whoa that was close!"*

Student A *says, "Thanks for saving me! That was fast thinking!"*

Student B *says, "No problem!" and they continue to walk home.*

The end.

Ask:

Were the students in danger? Yes! Did Student B's amygdala help them be safer? Yes! What choice did the amygdala make in that moment? That's right — flight! No, they didn't fly away but they moved quickly to avoid the bike.

Would it have helped if Student B got angry and tried to fight the bike? No!

Would it have helped if Student B had frozen and just stared at the bike? No!

Say: *So sometimes our amygdala can be really helpful and sometimes it needs a little help from us. Next time we'll learn about another part of our brain.*

Kindness Pals

Invite students to share what they did for their pals over the last week.

Assign new Kindness Pals after they are finished sharing.

 Kindness Pal Activity: Sharing

Say: *Ask your Kindness Pal to tell you about a time when their amygdala either protected them or made things worse.*

Closing words: *Okay, our time is up for today. Thank you for a great class, everyone. Let's have a nice quiet moment for the bell. If you want to, you can close your eyes, picture your new Kindness Pal, and imagine yourself doing something kind for them this week.*

Ring the bell.

Week 23
Who's the Boss? (Prefrontal Cortex)

MINDFULNESS PRACTICE: Choice of Take Five Breathing, Gravity Hands, Four Square Breathing

OBJECTIVES: Learn about how three parts of our brain, the amygdala — hippocampus, and prefrontal cortex — operate in regulating our emotions and reactions to stimuli.

Practice kindness.

PREPARE: A bell or chime

Diagram of the brain found in Resource Section

Your Kindness Pals list

Optional: Talking Object

In the last lesson, we learned about the role of the amygdala. This week's focus is on our Prefrontal Cortex, or PFC, the part of the brain that helps us make good decisions about how to respond in challenging situations. Students learn how mindfulness can calm the amygdala and put the PFC back in charge. We'll start this lesson with student-choice mindfulness practice. You might check in with your students to see which practices are helping them most!

Mindfulness Practice

Invite today's Mindfulness Helper (MH) to come to the front of the class to sit next to you on a chair (or next to you on the floor).

Say: *Let's all be happy for _____. (sign language applause)*

Say: *Today you'll get to choose which mindfulness practice you'd like to do. You can choose from Take Five Breathing, Four Square Breathing, and Gravity Hands. When the Mindfulness Helper says "Let's take three deep breaths" you can decide what you'd like to do.*

Prompt the MH to say: "Let's get into our mindful bodies. Let's close our eyes or look down. Let's take three deep breaths."

Say: *After you are done taking your deep breaths, let your breath settle back into its natural rhythm. Just breathe in and out normally. Put a hand on your tummy and see if you can make the rest of your body so still that the only thing that you feel moving is your breath.*

Wait about 30 seconds.

Say: *In a moment you will hear the sound of the bell. When you hear that sound, it will be time to open your eyes if they are closed.*

Ask the MH to ring the bell when the mindful breathing is complete and return to their seat.

Brain Science: Meet Your Prefrontal Cortex

Say: *Last time we learned about the amygdala. Does anybody remember what the amygdala's job is? That's right — your amygdala wants to keep you safe. But humans have evolved to keep up with the changing world and our brains have evolved too.*

Over a very long time — hundreds of millions of years — human beings grew a new, very important part of our brains called the Prefrontal Cortex.

Fold your fingers back down.

This part (pointing to your folded-over fingers) *is called the Prefrontal Cortex. You can call it the PFC for short.*

Your Prefrontal Cortex is the part of your brain that helps you to make good decisions. It helps you think things over and imagine what will happen.

Flipping Your Lid

Say: *Imagine that you are having a playdate with a friend. You have a new Monopoly game and you can't wait to play. You've been looking forward to playing Monopoly all day.*

When your friend arrives she says that she has been cooped up inside all day and can't wait to go out to play soccer.

Ask the class:

- How do you feel? (Angry, upset, disappointed.)
- What does your amygdala tell you to do? (Cry, yell, tell her that if you can't play Monopoly, you'll hold your breath until you turn blue…)
- How will things turn out if you only listen to your amygdala? (Your friend will be mad, might go home, won't want to play with you anymore….)

Observe: *When we feel like that, it's as if we've flipped our lid.*

Flip your fingers up exposing the amygdala.

Say: *It can feel like our amygdala is in charge, and we can't think very well because our Prefrontal Cortex or PFC is no longer working. You really need your Prefrontal Cortex (or PFC) to help you work this out. But how can you get it back in charge again?*

When we take our deep breaths and take care of our anger, it helps to bring our Prefrontal Cortex back in charge.

Fold your fingers down slowly.

Say: *It can take a little while to work, but once we have our lids back on we can think about what we want to do. We have choices.*

Once you have your lid back on and your PFC is in charge, you can think about how much you like your friend, and you start to think about your options.

Ask: *What are some other ways to solve this problem?* (Take turns playing soccer and Monopoly, let your guest decide what to play, and so on.)

Do you see how your PFC helps you see that you have choices and sometimes what your amygdala wants you to do isn't always the best idea?

Managing Our Anger

Say: *The next time you get angry, see if you can remember that this is your amygdala talking to you. See if you can use your breathing to help take care of your amygdala.*

It's important to remember that your amygdala is trying to take care of you. If you feel angry or upset that is fine. All of your emotions are fine.

The problem with anger is that sometimes the way we express it can make things worse for us and for those around us.

Once you have calmed down, you can figure out the best way to express what is bothering you so that you can take care of it.

Remember, we are not trying to get rid of our anger or any of our emotions. We're just trying to make sure that our feelings aren't controlling us.

Focus Practice: Exercise your PFC with Walk, Stop, Wiggle, Sit

Say: *Remember when we played this game back in Week 16? We're going to do it again here. Walk, Stop, Wiggle, Sit is a great game to challenge your PFC because your PFC is the part of your brain that is in charge of making decisions and organizing the rest of your brain and body into action. There are other parts of your brain that are in charge of listening and movements but they need the PFC to put it all together. Of course we know that the PFC is in charge unless the amygdala decides that you are in danger and takes over. So we're going to try to stay focused and calm in order to be able to do these increasingly hard levels of the game.*

Here's how to play. There are many levels of this game.

Give directions to play Walk, Stop, Wiggle, Sit.

We're going to play the game without talking so that everyone can hear the directions.

- You won't get "out" if you make a mistake. Just keep trying.
- Make sure that you are not talking and that you are not touching anybody else.

For this first round,

- When I say Walk, you are going to walk.
- When I say Stop, you are going to stop.
- When I say Wiggle, you are going to wiggle.
- When I say Sit, you are going to sit down. Got it?

Level 1:

Walk = Walk

Stop = Stop

Wiggle = Wiggle

Sit = Sit

Try it a few times, changing the order and timing of the commands.

Level 2:

Say: *This time we're going to switch things up. When I say Walk you are going to Stop. When I say Stop you are going to Walk. When I say Wiggle you are still going to Wiggle. When I say Sit you are still going to Sit. Okay?*

Walk = Stop

Stop = Walk

Wiggle = Wiggle

Sit = Sit

Try it a few times, changing the order and timing of the commands.

Level 3:

Say: *Okay now I'm going to make it a little harder. This time when I say Walk you are going to Stop. When I say Stop you are going to Walk. When I say Wiggle you are going to Sit and when I saw Sit you are going to Wiggle.*

Walk = Stop

Stop = Walk

Wiggle = Sit

Sit = Wiggle

Try it a few times, changing the order and timing of the commands.

Note: You can make many more variations of this game — adding more levels, letting students lead the game, adding in different movements, etc. Have fun! Start out with a few levels and then add on more each time you play it.

Kindness Pals

Invite students to share what they did for their pals over the last week.

Assign new Kindness Pals after they are finished sharing.

Kindness Pals Activity: Mirror Game

Say: *Now we're going to play a game with our new Kindness Pal that we played a few weeks ago with a different partner. We are going to be moving mindfully and really focusing on what our Kindness Pal is doing.*

Say: *We're going to play the Mirror Game. You are going to take turns being the leader and doing slow movements with your body. Your Kindness Pal will try to be your reflection in the mirror and do the exact same movements. After one minute I will ask you to switch and the other person will be the leader.*

You can demonstrate with a student so that they get the idea.

Instruct the children to stand up facing their new Kindness Pal. Ask them to be mindful of other people's bodies when they choose their space. Use this as an opportunity to model moving mindfully.

Ask the children to choose the first leader and when you say "Go" the leader starts doing slow movements and the other person tries to follow those movements. Give them a minute or more and then say "Switch" and have them switch roles.

Encourage the children to focus on what their bodies feel like when they are moving.

You might say: *Notice how heavy your arms feel when you hold them out in front of you.*

When you are finished you can ask the students to share what it felt like to play the game. What was easy? What was hard about it?

Closing words: *Okay our time is up for today. Thank you for a great class, everyone.*

Let's have a nice quiet moment for the bell. If you want to, you can close your eyes, picture your new Kindness Pal, and imagine yourself doing something kind for them this week.

Ring the bell.

Week 24
Do You Remember? (Hippocampus)

MINDFULNESS PRACTICE: Take Five Breathing

OBJECTIVES: Understand how three parts of our brain — the amygdala, hippocampus, and prefrontal cortex — operate in regulating our emotions and reactions to stimuli.

Practice kindness.

PREPARE: A bell or chime

Copies of the *Rosie's Brain* Skit from the Resource Section

Your Kindness Pals list

Today we'll learn more about the third part of the brain that relates to mindfulness and big emotions: the hippocampus. Our memories about how to meet challenges with skill and compassion aren't accessible when our amygdala is controlling the show. Our skit today, Rosie's Brain, helps students understand that when they are able to use mindfulness to calm their amygdala, they are able to access memories stored in the hippocampus that can be helpful in finding a good solution to a problem. Enjoy!

Mindfulness Practice

Invite today's Mindfulness Helper (MH) to come to the front of the class to sit next to you on a chair.

Say: *Let's all be happy for _____.* (sign language applause)

Prompt the MH to say: "Let's get into our mindful bodies. Let's close our eyes. Let's take five deep breaths."

Say: *Let's practice our Take Five Breathing. Trace your hand while you breathe in and out five times.*

Say: *Now take a deep breath, and listen for the sound of the bell. When you hear that sound it will be time to open your eyes.*

Ask the MH to ring the bell and return to their seat.

Brain Science: Introduce the Hippocampus

You might say:

In this lesson we will be adding to our knowledge of the brain by learning about the hippocampus. Do you remember last time when we learned about two parts of our brains?

Can anybody remember what they were called or what they did? (The amygdala and the prefrontal cortex.)

Review the jobs of the amygdala and the PFC.

You might continue by saying:

Well there are lots of other parts of your brain. Today we are going to learn about the hippocampus. The hippocampus is like a big storage cabinet or a library inside of your brain. It is the part of the brain that stores all of your memories.

Can anybody tell me what you had for breakfast today? (Let someone answer.)

Well that memory was stored in your hippocampus! Have you ever been to the beach? Eaten a pepper? Touched a snake? (Let kids raise their hands if they have done any of those things.)

So when I asked those questions your brains went looking in the hippocampus for the answer. Some of us found it, but some of us didn't because it was not there. Sometimes you forget something and that means that it was a little harder for your hippocampus to find it.

Act it Out: Rosie's Brain

Depending on the reading levels of your students you can do this skit in the manner of the role-plays in earlier lessons: you can read them aloud and have the students do the actions and repeat their lines after you read them aloud.

If your students can handle reading the scripts, you can hand out scripts, give the kids a little time to preview their lines, and then you can just be the director.

Feel free to modify the story or change the names to fit the needs of your class.

Today we are going to act out a skit that illustrates how these three parts of our brains work. This skit was the basis for the book Rosie's Brain *that we read in Week 21.*

Choose students to act out the Brain Skit found in the Resource Section. You might act out the skit two or three times with different actors.

Reflect and Discuss

You might launch a discussion with these questions.
- Why was Rosie angry?
- What did her Amygdala (Amy) want her to do?
- How did her Hippocampus (Miss Pickles) help her?
- How did her PFC help her?
- Can you think of another solution to her problem?

Kindness Pals

Invite students to share what they did for their pals over the last week.

Assign new Kindness Pals after they are finished sharing.

 Kindness Pals Activity: Hippocampus Workout

Have students sit with their Kindness pal and ask each other five questions: favorite color, favorite food, favorite pizza topping, favorite time of day, and favorite animal. Take turns answering the questions.

Then see if they can repeat back all of their Kindness Pal's answers, taking turns. If they manage that, then they can think of five more questions and try to remember all ten answers. Help them give their hippocampus a workout!

Closing words: *Okay our time is up for today. Thank you for a great class, everyone. Let's have a nice quiet moment for the bell. If you want to, you can close your eyes, picture your new Kindness Pal, and imagine yourself doing something kind for them this week.*

Ring the bell

UNIT 7: Conflict Resolution

Week 25
Learn about Conflict with Zion and Zuri

MINDFULNESS PRACTICE: Squeeze and Release

OBJECTIVES: Learn what conflict means.

Practice kindness.

PREPARE: A bell or chime

Fun Saturday by Linda Ryden (included in the lesson)

Your Kindness Pals list

Welcome to our unit on Conflict Resolution! All of the lessons since Week 1 have been building to this unit, which would not be nearly as helpful without the foundation you have built with your students to this point. We strongly believe that mindfulness, empathy, and kindness practice together with a basic understanding of brain science create the necessary foundation for skillful, compassionate conflict resolution. Today students will get to learn about conflict through a role play. We will use skits in nearly every lesson of this unit to help students begin to internalize positive, skillful ways of working out conflicts. Have fun!

Mindfulness Practice

Say: *Today we're going to try Squeeze and Release again.* (Remind them how to do this practice from Week 16).

Invite today's Mindfulness Helper (MH) to come to the front of the class to sit next to you on a chair (or next to you on the floor).

Say: *Let's all be happy for _____.* (sign language applause)

Prompt the MH to say: "Let's get into our mindful bodies. Let's close our eyes or look down. Let's do Squeeze and Release."

You or the Mindfulness Helper can lead the class through the practice again.

Ask the MH to ring the bell when the mindful breathing is complete and return to their seat.

Conflict Resolution: What is Conflict?

You might say: *Today we are going to learn a word that might be new to some of you.*

Ask the class:

- Has anybody ever heard the word **Conflict** before?
- Does anybody have a guess about what it means?

Say: *In our Mindfulness lessons, we've been learning about what happens in our brains when we get angry. Well, sometimes when we are angry, it is because we have a conflict.*

A conflict can be any kind of small problem. Maybe you are having a playdate and you want to play outside but your friend wants to play inside. Maybe your little brother wants to play with you, but you want to read.

Conflicts can stay small or they can get bigger. Can anyone give an example of a conflict?

Take a few answers.

Today we are going to act out a conflict. I'm going to choose two kids to act out the story about a brother and sister named Zion and Zuri.

Act it Out: Fun Saturday (1)

Choose two kids to act out the story and ask them to pantomime what you are describing in the story — if you say they are jumping up and down the kids will jump up and down.

You will be the narrator and you will read their lines and then the kids can repeat the lines after you read them.

Here is the script to read aloud.

Narrator: *Every Saturday morning Zuri and Zion go to the park.* **Zuri** *and* **Zion** *LOVE Saturday mornings!*

They love to play basketball. (act out playing basketball) *They love to go on the swings.* (act out playing on the swings, etc.) *They love to climb trees. They love to ride bikes. They love to count ladybugs. They love to play in the water fountain. They love to do the monkey bars.*

Have the kids suggest more things for Zion and Zuri to do at the park and have the kids act them out.

Last week **Zuri** *was able to get all the way across the monkey bars for the first time and she really wanted to do it again this week.*

But **Zion** *had been dreaming about splashing in the fountain all during this hot week.*

Zuri *said, "Let's go to the monkey bars! I can't wait to try going all the way across!"*

Zion *said, "No! I'm hot! I want to splash in the fountain!"*

Zuri *said, "But Mom said we have to stay together! And I want to go to the monkey bars!" Zuri was starting to get frustrated now. Her face was getting hot and her body felt tight and tense.*

Zion *was angry. He always had to watch his younger sister and sometimes it made him feel frustrated. He could feel that frustrated feeling in his belly. He said, "The monkey bars are boring! I've been going across since I was 6 years old!"*

Zuri *was really mad now. She said, "You're a show-off! Big brothers are the worst!"*

Zion *was angry too. He said, "No, you're the worst!"*

Zuri *said, "What?! I'm going to tell Mom that you're the meanest brother ever!"*

Zion *said, "Fine with me!"*

They both stormed off and sat on separate benches for the rest of the morning.

The End.

Discuss and Reflect

Spark a discussion with these questions:

- What is the conflict between Zion and Zuri?
- How can you tell that they are getting angry? (Body language, yelling.)
- What part of Zuri and Zion's brains are controlling their actions? (Amygdala.)
- Has their amygdala chosen fight, flight, or freeze?
- How is that choice working out for them?
- What part of their brains would help them work this conflict out peacefully? (The prefrontal cortex.)
- If they were using their PFCs, how could they solve this conflict?

Take a few answers.

Act it Out: Fun Saturday (2)

Introduce the Role Play again.

You might say: *Now we are going to act out the story of Zion and Zuri again but we are going to write new endings to the story.*

Choose two new volunteers to be Zuri and Zion.

Invite the volunteers to act out the story as you read. Freeze the action at various points to ask the class for suggestions about how to solve their conflicts.

If they don't suggest it, offer these ideas:

- They could take turns playing on the monkey bars and then the fountain.
- One of them could just offer to do what the other one wants to do out of simple kindness.
- They could compromise and do something else, like play on the swings.

Ask: *Would things have turned out better for the Zuri and Zion if they had tried any of our ideas?*

Kindness Pals

Invite students to share what they did for their pals over the last week.

Assign new Kindness Pals after they are finished sharing.

 Kindness Pals Activity: Hippocampus Workout

Have students sit with their Kindness pal and ask each other five questions: favorite color, favorite food, favorite pizza topping, favorite time of day, and favorite animal. Take turns answering the questions.

Then see if they can repeat back all of their Kindness Pal's answers, taking turns. If they manage that, then they can think of five more questions and try to remember all ten answers. Help them give their hippocampus a workout!

Closing words: *Okay our time is up for today. Thank you for a great class, everyone. Let's have a nice quiet moment for the bell. If you want to, you can close your eyes, picture your new Kindness Pal, and imagine yourself doing something kind for them this week.*

Ring the bell

Week 26
The Conflict Escalator

MINDFULNESS PRACTICE: Take Five Breathing

OBJECTIVES: Use the concept of a Conflict Escalator, developed and named by William Kreidler, to help children understand how and why conflicts get worse.

Practice kindness

PREPARE: A bell or chime

Copies of the *Scrabble vs. Monopoly* Skits for all students (See Resource Section)

Your Kindness Pals list

Optional: Talking Object

The first step to resolving a conflict is recognizing when we are in one and when it is escalating. In this lesson, we will use the concept of a Conflict Escalator, developed and named by William Kreidler, to help children understand how and why conflicts get worse. This is a key step in learning how to de-escalate and peacefully resolve conflicts.

Mindfulness Practice

Say: *Today we're going to do Take Five Breathing.*

Invite today's Mindfulness Helper (MH) to come to the front of the class to sit next to you on a chair (or next to you on the floor).

Say: *Let's all be happy for _____.* (sign language applause)

Prompt the MH to say: "Let's get into our mindful bodies. Let's close our eyes or look down. Let's take five deep breaths."

You or the Mindfulness Helper can lead the class through the practice again.

Ask the MH to ring the bell when the mindful breathing is complete and return to their seat.

Conflict Resolution Practice

You might say: *Today we are going to continue talking about conflicts. Remember the story of Zion and Zuri?*

Ask:

- What was their conflict about?
- Did their conflict stay small or did it get bigger?
- What made their conflict get bigger?

One way to think about how conflicts get bigger is called the Conflict Escalator.

Draw an escalator on the board. See the Resource Section for a blank escalator that you may fill in. Refer to the image at the end of this lesson for an example.

Ask the children to describe what an escalator does.

Explain that when conflict gets worse, we say that the people involved are going up the Conflict Escalator.

Point out how Zion and Zuri went up the Conflict Escalator.

Act it Out: Scrabble vs. Monopoly 1

Depending on the reading levels of your students you can do this skit in the manner of the role-plays in earlier lessons: you can read them aloud and have the students do the actions and repeat their lines after you read them aloud.

If your students can handle reading the scripts, you can hand out scripts, give the kids a little time to preview their lines, and then just be the director.

Feel free to modify the story or change the names to fit the needs of your class.

Hand out copies of the Scrabble vs. Monopoly 1 Skit found in the Resource Section.

Say: *Today we are going to act out a skit about kids who are having a conflict. It's called Scrabble vs. Monopoly.*

We will need six actors. They will be: Charlie, Henry, Julio, Lucy, Reign, and Alice.

Choose actors and give them a minute to review their lines.

Act out Scrabble vs. Monopoly 1.

NOTE FROM LINDA: *The "main characters", Charlie and Lucy, have more lines than the others. I like to write in smaller parts for kids who might be more reluctant readers. Julio would be a good part for a more hesitant reader and he becomes the "hero" at the end so that's nice!*

Reflect and Discuss

Ask: *Has this ever happened to you? You're having a good time and then suddenly everything gets out of control and goes totally wrong?*

Take a few answers.

Say: *Sometimes a conflict, problem, or argument can get worse and worse, and people start saying mean things, yelling, or even hitting each other. We call that going up the Conflict Escalator.*

Questions for discussion:

- What was their conflict about?
- What was the first thing that made their conflict escalate or go up the Conflict Escalator?
- Then what happened? Let's map the conflict on the Conflict Escalator.
- What could these kids have done differently to avoid going up the Conflict Escalator?
- How could they work out this conflict?
- What part of their brains are driving their reactions? (Amygdala.)
- Did the characters in the skit "flip their lids"? Give examples.

Act it Out: Scrabble vs. Monopoly 2

You might say: *Now let's act out another version of this skit and see what happens.*

Choose actors and give them a minute to review their lines.

Act out Scrabble vs. Monopoly 2.

Reflect and Discuss

You might ask:

- Do you think that was a good way to work out their conflict?
- Was it better than going up the Conflict Escalator?

Say: *When people go up the Conflict Escalator someone always gets hurt. Either their feelings get hurt or they get hurt physically.*

Ask:

- How did the kids calm down? (Breathing.)
- Did taking those deep breaths help them to quiet their amygdalas?
- What part of their brains was in charge when they worked out the conflict peacefully? (Prefrontal cortex.)
- What else did they do to bring their conflict down the Escalator? (Apologize.)

Say: *Okay, next time we are going to act out another skit about the Conflict Escalator.*

Kindness Pals

Invite students to share what they did for their pals over the last week.

Assign new Kindness Pals after they are finished sharing.

Kindness Pals Activity: Marble Game Repeat

Say: *Remember when we read* Sergio Sees the Good? *We're going to play that marble game again today.*

I'm going to give you and your Kindness Pal two cups and some marbles (or pasta, paperclips, whatever you have). *You are going to sit across from each other with the cups in between you. You can choose one cup to be the Good cup and one cup to be the Bad cup.*

Then you are going to decide who goes first. That person will be the talker and the other person will hold the marbles. The talker will try to remember everything that happened yesterday and the marble holder will put marbles in the good cup for good things and in the bad cup for bad things. At the end you can count how many marbles are in each cup. Then you will switch places. Try to remember lots of little details.

Give them about 5-10 minutes for this. This is a powerful practice because not only are they thinking about and remembering little good things but they are really listening to each other and witnessing each other's lives.

When the time is up ask the kids to reflect on how many good and bad marbles they had in each cup and what it felt like to do the activity.

Closing: *Okay our time is up for today. Thank you for a great class, everyone. Let's have a nice quiet moment for the bell. If you want to, you can close your eyes, picture your new Kindness Pal, and imagine yourself doing something kind for them this week.*

Ring the bell.

Week 27
Conflict Escalator Practice: The Class Party

MINDFULNESS PRACTICE: Gravity Hands, Heartfulness

OBJECTIVES: Reinforce the concept of the Conflict Escalator.

Practice kindness.

PREPARE: A bell or chime

Copies of the skits *The Class Party 1* and *The Class Party 2* found in Resource Section

Your Kindness Pals list

Optional: Talking Object

Often when we are in a conflict, it's hard for us to think clearly about the person we are mad at. Our mindfulness practice for the day, Heartfulness, can help us to empathize with the person we are in a conflict with, making it easier to find a solution. Today kids will have another chance to practice with the Conflict Escalator. Practicing together in class helps children build a common language and set of tools to use outside of the classroom.

Mindfulness Practice

Say: *Today we are going to start out by practicing Heartfulness. This just means that we are going to be thinking about a person and sending them kind thoughts. We did this a while back so you might remember it.*

Invite the day's Mindfulness Helper (MH) to come to the front of the class to sit next to you on a chair.

Prompt the MH to say: "Let's get into our mindful bodies. Let's close our eyes. Let's take three deep breaths with Gravity Hands."

Say: *I'd like you to think about someone who makes you happy. Choose someone you see every day, at home or at school. It could be someone in your family, a friend, a teacher, even a pet. Just choose someone and try to picture this person happy and smiling. Picture them doing something that makes them happy. Try to notice how you feel when you think about this person.*

Now, if you'd like to, fill your heart up with kindness and repeat these words in your mind while you think about this person:

May you be happy. **Wait a moment.**

May you be healthy. **Wait a moment.**

May you be peaceful. **Wait a moment.**

Take a moment to notice how you feel. Any way that you feel is fine, even if you feel nothing. Just try to notice it.

Introduce a new focus: *Now we are going to try this again but this time we are going to send kind thoughts to someone that we are a little bit mad at or someone we had a little conflict with. We're not going to think about somebody that we are really mad at, just someone we're a little bit annoyed at. This might be harder but just try it and see what happens. If you can't think of anyone you can just choose another person — maybe somebody that you don't know very well.*

Now, if you'd like to, fill your heart up with kindness and repeat these words in your mind while you think about this person:

May you be happy. **Wait a moment.**

May you be healthy. **Wait a moment.**

May you be peaceful. **Wait a moment.**

Take a moment to notice how you feel. Any way that you feel is fine, even if you feel nothing. Just try to notice it.

Say: *Now let's take one more deep breath in and out. In a moment you will hear the sound of the bell and that will mean that it is time to open your eyes.*

Ask the MH to ring the bell when the mindful breathing is complete.

Ask the MH to return to their seat.

Invite the students to share what it was like to send kind thoughts in your mind to someone you are angry with or in a conflict with.

Important: Ask them not to share the name of the person they were thinking about if it is someone at school.

Conflict Resolution Practice

You might say: *In our last class we learned about the Conflict Escalator. Does anybody remember what that is?*

Take a few answers.

We acted out a skit about kids having a conflict about what game to play.

Today we are going to act out another skit about a conflict. It's called The Class Party.

I will be choosing some people to play the parts in the skit.

I want the rest of you to pay close attention and every time you notice somebody doing or saying something that causes the conflict to escalate or go up the Conflict Escalator I want you to point up. When you notice somebody doing something that causes the conflict to go down the Conflict Escalator, point down.

Act it Out: The Class Party Skit 1

We will need five actors. They will be: Richard, Leslie, Frankie, Diana, and Oscar.

Choose Actors.

The Scene is a school classroom during indoor recess.

Hand out copies of the *Class Party 1* Skit. Give students a few moments to get familiar with their lines.

Act out Class Party 1.

Model pointing up or down as actors go up and down the Conflict Escalator.

Reflect and Discuss

You might say: *Does this sound familiar? You're just talking and then everything gets out of control. Sometimes you're not even sure what happened. All you know is that you're mad.*

Ask:

- What was their conflict about? What happened that caused their conflict to escalate, get worse, or go up the Conflict Escalator?
- What part of the brain is responsible for making us go up the Conflict Escalator?
- Are these kids being mindful of what they are saying? What did you think they should do to try to bring their conflict down the Conflict Escalator?

Now we're going to act out another version of this skit. Let's see what happens when they try things a different way.

Act it Out: The Class Party Skit 2

You might say: *Now let's act out another version of this skit and see what happens:*

Choose actors and give them a minute to review their lines.

Act out Class Party 2.

Remind the audience to point up when actors are going up the Conflict Escalator, and to point down when they are going down.

Reflect and Discuss

Ask: *Do you think that was a good way to work out their conflict? What is another idea? What else did you notice that they did to bring their conflict down?*

Next time we are going to be talking about apologizing.

Kindness Pals

Invite students to share what they did for their pals over the last week.

Assign new Kindness Pals after they are finished sharing.

Kindness Pals Activity: Nine Words

Say: *Let's try the Nine Words Challenge again with your new Kindness Pal. Today you and your new Kindness Pals will have a challenge. You're going to try to come up with nine words that start with the first letter of each one of your names. We've done food, animals, free for all…Let's think of three new categories.*

Take their answers and play the game as before (see Week 10).

After 5-10 minutes give them a chance to share some of their answers with the class.

Closing: *Okay our time is up for today. Thank you for a great class, everyone. Let's have a nice quiet moment for the bell. If you want to, you can close your eyes, picture your new Kindness Pal, and imagine yourself doing something kind for them this week.*

Ring the bell.

Week 28
MOFL or Awful?

MINDFULNESS PRACTICE: Guided Reflection

OBJECTIVES: Understand what makes a good apology.
Practice apologizing.
Practice kindness.

PREPARE: A bell or chime
Your Kindness Pals list

A critical component of successful, peaceful conflict resolution is a good apology. Apologizing can be challenging and takes practice. When we start with mindfulness to calm anger, apologizing is more accessible. In this lesson we explore the four components of a good apology: Mean it, Own it, Fix it, and then Let it Go. Note: in this lesson we assign new Kindness Pals earlier than usual. If you can, save a few moments at the end for students to share their kind acts from the last week.

Mindfulness Practice

You might say: *Today we are going to focus on apologizing. Apologizing is an important part of working out conflicts. If you have gone up the Conflict Escalator, then you have most likely done or said something that you need to apologize for. Today we are going to be thinking about what makes a good apology. After we do our Gravity Hands breathing, I am going to ask you to think about a time when an apology would have been helpful.*

Invite today's Mindfulness Helper (MH) to come to the front of the class to sit next to you on a chair.

Say: *Let's all be happy for _____.* (sign language applause)

Prompt the MH to say: "Let's get into our mindful bodies. Let's close our eyes or look down. Let's take three deep breaths with Gravity Hands."

Say: *Let's keep our eyes closed or down. I'd like you to try to remember a time when you did something that hurt somebody else's feelings. It happens to all of us. Try to remember a time.* **Pause.**

How did you feel? What did you do about it? Did you say you were sorry? Was that hard? **Pause.**

If you didn't say you were sorry, try saying it now. You can whisper it or say it inside your mind. **Pause.**

Say: *Now let's take one more deep breath in and out. In a moment you will hear the sound of the bell and that will mean that it is time to open your eyes or look up.*

Ask the MH to ring the bell and return to their seat.

Reflect and Discuss

Ask: *Does anybody want to share what you were thinking about?*

Ask: *Is it hard to say you're sorry? Why do you think it can be so hard?*

You might say:

When two or more people go up the conflict escalator, everyone involved has done something to escalate the conflict. You can't go up the conflict escalator alone.

In order to come to a fair and long-lasting solution, it is important that everyone take responsibility for their actions and their part in making the conflict escalate.

The act of apologizing for whatever you did, such as "I'm sorry I called you a name" or "I'm sorry I criticized your idea," can clear the air and make it much easier for you to see the other person's point of view and find a fair solution.

Apologizing Practice 1

We introduce the concept of MOFL — Mean it, Own it, Fix It, Let it Go — to help students understand what makes a good apology. Here's a skit-based approach to explaining MOFL.

Choose one student to act with you.

Invite the student to stand next to you and hold a bunch of tissue boxes, markers, or things that won't get broken when dropped.

Walk over and gently bump the student so that they drop what they are holding.

Prompt the student to say, "Hey! You made me drop my stuff!"

Act out these four apology scenarios:

1. You say, "Sorry!" and keep walking.

Ask: Is that a good apology? Why or why not? **Take a few answers**.

2. Act it out again but this time say, "Sorry! I needed to get by" and keep walking.

Ask: Is that a good apology? Why or why not? **Take a few answers**.

3. Act it out again but this time say, "Oh no! I'm so sorry! I wasn't watching where I was going. Can I help you pick up your stuff? I'm really sorry."

Ask: Is that a good apology? Why or why not? **Take a few answers.**

4. Act it out again but this time say, "Oh no! I'm so sorry! I wasn't watching where I was going. Can I help you pick up your stuff? I'm really sorry. Do you forgive me? You have to forgive me! I said I was sorry! Tell me that it's okay!"

Ask: Is that a good apology? Why or why not? **Take a few answers.**

Now write on the board **M O F L.**

Ask if anyone can guess what the letters stand for. Give them the hint that it has something to do with apologizing.

Explain that the **M stands for Mean it**. A good apology has to be sincere and the person receiving it should see that you are truly sorry.

Ask: *What was wrong with saying, "Sorry I needed to get by"? Why wasn't that a good apology?*

Somebody will probably say because the person didn't take responsibility for what they did. The **O in MOFL stands for Own it.** You have to take responsibility for what you did. Rather than saying "Mistakes were made" we would say "I made a mistake." In this case they could have said, "I was trying to get by but I bumped into you. I'm sorry!"

Ask: *When I offered to pick up the stuff you dropped, what was I trying to do?* (trying to fix it)

The **F stands for Fix it.** Even though it's not always possible, it's important to try to make amends and see if there is anything you can do to fix or remedy the situation.

Ask: *In the fourth apology I was begging you to forgive me. Was the fourth apology a good one? Why or why not?*

The **L stands for Let it Go**. Sometimes when people apologize they get very upset if the person receiving their apology doesn't accept it. It's important to remember that sometimes people aren't ready to forgive. Maybe they are still upset about what happened, even if they aren't really mad at you. We need to offer apologies and then let it go and let the person come to forgiveness when and if they are ready.

Ask: *So, what are the four important parts of a good apology?* **Mean it, Own it, Fix it, Let it go = MOFL.**

Mean it: show the person that you really regret what happened. Ask for an example.

Own it: In the skit I didn't bump into the student on purpose. Do you have to take responsibility for what you did even if it was an accident? Ask for an example.

Fix it: what can you do to make things right? Ask for an example.

Let it Go: don't chase the person around making them forgive you. Sometimes that takes time — that isn't what this is about. This is about you offering something to the other person. You can't make them take it. But you do the right thing anyway. The only person you can control is yourself. Ask for an example.

Apologizing Practice 2

You might say: *Today you're going to work with your Kindness Pal to create some apologies. You will decide on a scenario — like when I bumped into (student's name) and caused them to drop their stuff. Then you will demonstrate three "awful" apologies and then one "MOFL" apology. Remember that MOFL stands for Mean it, Own it, Fix it, and Let it Go.*

Here are the rules for these skits. You may not touch each other and no inappropriate language. Make sure you take turns so that you each get to practice apologizing.

After five minutes ask for a few volunteers to share their apologies and have the class decide if they are MOFL or Awful.

Kindness Pals

Invite students to share what they did for their pals over the last week.

Assign new Kindness Pals after they are finished sharing.

 Kindness Pal Activity: Kindness Pal Challenge

Say: *I'm going to set a timer for 90 seconds. You're going to sit with your new Kindness Pal and try to find out how many things you two have in common. Remember to ask each other questions and keep track. When I ring the bell, we'll share what we found out about each other.*

You can let the time go longer than 90 seconds if the kids seem to be having a good time.

Share. Come back together as a group and ask them to share something that they learned about their Kindness Pals. This exercise is a great way to practice Mindful Listening and help them to develop an interest in others.

If you have time, invite students to share the kind things they did for their old Kindness Pals in the last week.

Closing words: *Okay our time is up for today. Thank you for a great class, everyone. Let's have a nice quiet moment for the bell. If you want to, you can close your eyes, picture your new Kindness Pal, and imagine yourself doing something kind for them this week.*

Ring the bell.

Week 29
The Conflict C.A.T.

MINDFULNESS PRACTICE: Blooming Breaths

OBJECTIVES: Introduce the Conflict C.A.T.

Practice kindness.

PREPARE: A bell or chime

Copy of the Conflict C.A.T. for the classroom (see Resource Section)

Your Kindness Pals list

Optional: Talking Object

The Conflict C.A.T. is shorthand for the Peace of Mind Conflict Resolution Method: Calm Down, Apologize, and Toolbox. Your students now have many mindfulness skills to help them with Step 1: Calm Down. Today you will have a chance to help your students apply these skills to using a few different conflict resolution tools to de-escalate and solve conflicts. The more students practice using these tools when they are not really necessary — i.e., through skits and role plays — the more likely it is that they will be able to call on them when they are really needed.

Mindfulness Practice

Say: *Today we're going to do Blooming Breaths again.* If needed, review Lesson 13.

Invite today's Mindfulness Helper (MH) to come to the front of the class to sit next to you on a chair (or next to you on the floor).

Say: *Let's all be happy for _____.* (sign language applause)

Prompt the MH to say: "Let's get into our mindful bodies. Let's close our eyes or look down. Let's take three deep Blooming Breaths."

Ask the MH to ring the bell when the mindful breathing is complete and return to their seat.

Conflict Resolution Practice

1. **Review**

   You might say: *So far we have learned about what conflict is and how it escalates or goes up the Conflict Escalator.*

   We've learned about what happens in our brains when we get angry — how we flip our lids and our amygdala takes over.

   In our mindfulness lessons, we've learned many ways to help us to calm down when we are angry. We've also learned about good ways to apologize.

   This is really powerful information that most people, including most grown-ups, don't have. With these tools we can make our own lives easier and make the world a more peaceful place.

2. **Introduce the Conflict C.A.T.**

   Today we are going to put all of these pieces together in a fun way that is easy to remember. I'd like to introduce you to the **Conflict C.A.T.***!*

   The Conflict C.A.T. stands for three of the most important things to do to work out a conflict:

   > C̲alm down
   > A̲pologize
   > T̲oolbox

   We've already learned about the first two parts. Today we are going to start to learn about what is in the Conflict Toolbox.

3. **Introduce the Toolbox: Taking Turns, Sharing, and Being Kind**

   Write "Conflict Toolbox" and then numbers 1-8 on the white board or chart paper. You'll be filling in the list as you go along in this lesson and the next one.

   Say: *Remember the skit we saw about the kids who were fighting over whether to play Monopoly or Scrabble?*

   Does anybody remember how they worked out their conflict?

Take a few answers. (They calmed down, they apologized, and then they decided to take turns.)

Taking turns *is one of the tools in the Conflict Toolbox.* (Write Take Turns on the Chart.) *Taking turns is a great tool to use and it works for a lot of conflicts. Let's say you need to use the classroom computer for a project, but someone is already using it to play a game. Would taking turns be a tool that would work to solve that conflict?*

What if you were planning to play basketball with your friends at recess, but when you get out to the playground some other kids are already there playing? Would taking turns work in that situation?

Sharing

What it if you and your brother really wanted to eat a cupcake, but there was only one cupcake left? Would taking turns work in that situation? First you eat the cupcake and then your brother eats it? Maybe not.

What would be a good tool to use in that situation? Yes, you could **share** *it.* (Write Share on the chart.)

Being Kind

*Or you could just let your brother eat the cupcake to be nice. That's a tool we call "**being kind**."* (Write Be Kind on the chart.)

So one tool doesn't work in every situation, but that's okay because there are a lot more!

4. **Using the Toolbox**

   Ask the class to apply these tools to different situations you suggest.

   You might say:

   Today we are going to focus on these three tools: **taking turns**, **sharing**, *and* **being kind**. *In our next lesson, we'll learn three more.*

   I'm going to choose some students to act out a conflict, and I want you to tell me which tool would work the best and why.

Choose students to briefly act out these situations and then ask the class which tools they could use to solve the conflict peacefully.

- Two kids are playing a game and they both want to go first.
- Two kids want to sit in the class rocking chair.
- You want to draw but somebody is already using all of the markers.
- Two kids can't agree on a movie to watch.

Kindness Pals

Invite students to share what they did for their pals over the last week.

Assign new Kindness Pals after they are finished sharing.

 Kindness Pals Activity: Kindness Pal Challenge

Say: *I'm going to set a timer for 90 seconds. You're going to sit with your new Kindness Pal and try to find out how many things are different about you. Favorite colors, foods, movies, etc. Remember to ask each other questions and keep track. When I ring the bell, we'll share what we found out about each other.*

You can let the time go longer than 90 seconds if the kids seem to be having a good time.

Share. Come back together as a group and ask them to share something that they learned about their Kindness Pals. This exercise is a great way to practice Mindful Listening and help them to develop an interest in others.

Closing words: *Okay, our time is up for today. Thank you for a great class, everyone. Let's have a nice quiet moment for the bell. If you want to, you can close your eyes, picture your new Kindness Pal, and imagine yourself doing something kind for them this week.*

Ring the bell.

Week 30
More about the Conflict Toolbox

MINDFULNESS PRACTICE: Your Choice

OBJECTIVES: Introduce more tools to help work out conflicts.

Practice kindness.

PREPARE: A bell or chime

Copies of the *Monopoly vs. Scrabble* 1 Skits from Resource Section

Your Kindness Pals list

Today students will have a chance to put the Conflict C.A.T. to work again. We will be re-visiting the skit your students acted out in Week 26, Monopoly vs. Scrabble 1. They will have a chance to decide which tools would work best to solve the conflict and act out their own ending for this skit. The more students can practice these skills, the more likely it will be that they can put them to work without always needing an adult to help.

Mindfulness Practice

Invite today's Mindfulness Helper (MH) to come to the front of the class to sit next to you on a chair.

Say: *Let's all be happy for _____.* (sign language applause)

Prompt the MH to say: "Let's get into our mindful bodies. Let's close our eyes. Let's take 3 deep breaths."

Ask students to consider which of the practices they have learned this year would be most helpful to them now. Suggest they practice that one.

Say: *Now let's take one more deep breath in and out. In a moment you will hear the sound of the bell and that will mean that it is time to open your eyes.*

Ask the MH to ring the bell and return to their seat.

Conflict Resolution Practice

1. **Review**

   You might say: Today we are going to learn about more of the tools in the Conflict C.A.T. Remember that the Conflict C.A.T. stands for the three most important things to do to work out a conflict: <u>C</u>alm down, <u>A</u>pologize, <u>T</u>oolbox.

   Last time we learned about three tools: **Share**, **Take Turns**, and **Be Kind**.

   There are eight tools in the Conflict Toolbox. There are so many other ways to work out conflicts, but these eight come in pretty handy. They are:

   1. Share
   2. Take Turns
   3. Be Kind
   4. Leave it to Chance
   5. Compromise
   6. Pause the Conflict
   7. Skip the Conflict
   8. Get Help

2. **Review each Tool**

   Share these descriptions of each tool with the class.

   Leave it to Chance

   <u>Leave it to Chance</u> might sound strange, but it's the one you've probably used the most. Leaving it to chance can mean flipping a coin; playing rock, paper, scissors; or something else like that.

   Leaving it to chance can be a great tool to use, but there are some drawbacks.

   What often happens when we flip a coin to work out a conflict? That's right, the person who loses the coin toss might say "Let's do best two out of three, or three out of five…."

   I suggest that when you use this tool, you check in with everyone first and make sure that everyone is okay with losing.

If you are having a conflict over something that is really important to you or over something that you have to do, this might not be the best tool to use. If you are having a conflict over who gets to use your family computer and you both have homework to do on the computer, is flipping a coin going to work? No, because then one of you won't get to do your homework. So we need more tools….

Compromise

Another important tool is <u>Compromise</u>. A compromise means that nobody in the conflict gets exactly what he or she wants, but both people agree on a solution in which they both get something good.

Let's say that you and your brother both want that last cookie in the cookie jar. A compromise would be that neither one of you eats the cookie, but that you eat some ice cream instead. As long as you both like ice cream, then that's a good compromise.

Pausing the Conflict

<u>Pausing the Conflict</u> means that you realize that you are going up the Conflict Escalator but that it is going to take you a bit longer to calm down enough to work out the conflict. Maybe you need to go to your room for a little while to do your mindful breathing. Maybe you need to go for a walk and count your steps and take care of your anger. Once you've calmed down, you can come back together and try to work things out.

Skip the Conflict

Sometimes a conflict just isn't worth going up the Conflict Escalator for. There is nothing but TROUBLE at the top of the Conflict Escalator. Once you have taken some deep breaths and calmed down a bit, you might realize that you are having a conflict about something silly. So you decide to <u>Skip the Conflict</u>.

This is a good tool to use also when you realize that you are doing your best to calm down and use the Conflict C.A.T., but you notice that the other person is still really angry and wanting to go up the Conflict Escalator. That would be a good time to walk away and <u>Skip the Conflict</u>.

Get Help

Sometimes when you are trying to work out a conflict you might need to <u>Get Help</u>. That means that you might ask a grown-up or a friend to help you work things out. Sometimes it's hard to see the solution when you are in the middle of something. If you are trying to be calm and work things out but the other person has flipped their lid, that would be a good time to <u>Get Help</u> too.

Act it Out: Scrabble vs. Monopoly Skit

You might say:

Do you remember the two skits that we acted out about conflicts? There was one about a group of kids arguing about playing Monopoly or Scrabble. There was one about a group of kids trying to come up with a theme for their class party.

Looking at the list of tools in the Conflict Toolbox, which tool did the kids use in the Monopoly skit? (Take turns.) *That's right, they decided to take turns and play Monopoly today and Scrabble tomorrow.*

What tool did the kids use in the class party skit? (Compromise.) *Since they all had different ideas for what the party should be, they came up with a compromise. They thought of something that they all cared about—the environment—and planned a party about that.*

What other tools would have worked in these conflicts? Let's act out the Monopoly skit again, but this time we are going to stop before they are done and see what other tool could work. We're going to read through the skit but then at the end I'm going to ask you to improvise or make up what the kids would say. Let's try it:

Note: Prompt them to use all of the tools in the toolbox.

Hand out copies of the *Scrabble vs. Monopoly* 1 Skit.

Choose 6 volunteers to play the roles of Charlie, Henry, Julio, Lucy, Reign, and Alice.

Charlie: Hey guys, let's play Monopoly! I just got a new game and I've been really wanting to play it.

Henry: That sounds great! I love Monopoly!

Julio: Yes! Monopoly is my favorite game!

Lucy: No way! Monopoly takes too long to play. Let's play Scrabble instead!

Reign: Yeah, Scrabble is awesome. I'm really good!

Alice: That's because you're a really good speller.

Reign: Thanks!

Charlie: What are you talking about? Monopoly is the coolest game. Scrabble is for geeks!

Lucy: Who are you calling a geek? You're a loser.

Henry: Hey you guys, we're going up the Conflict Escalator.

Reign: Oh, you're right. There's nothing but trouble at the top of the Conflict Escalator!

Julio: Why don't we calm down a bit? Let's do our Take Five Breathing.

Everybody stops and traces their hands and takes five deep breaths.

Lucy: Hey, Charlie, I'm sorry I called you a loser. I didn't mean it.

Charlie: No, I'm sorry. I shouldn't have said Scrabble is for geeks. I like Scrabble. I was just really excited to play Monopoly and I got carried away.

Alice: I have an idea!

STOP HERE

Discuss and Repeat

What tool in the toolbox would work to solve this conflict?

Take some ideas and then choose one to have the kids act out.

Talk about how it worked.

Repeat enough times to try out all the different tools.

Kindness Pals

Invite students to share what they did for their pals over the last week.

Assign new Kindness Pals after they are finished sharing.

♡ Kindness Pals Activity: Mirror Game

Say: *Today we're going to play the Mirror Game again with our new Kindness Pal. We are going to be moving mindfully and really focusing on what our Kindness Pal is doing. You are going to take turns being the leader and doing slow movements with your body. Your Kindness Pal will try to be your reflection in the mirror and do the exact same movements. After one minute I will ask you to switch and the other person will be the leader.* You can demonstrate with a student so that they get the idea.

Instruct the children to stand up facing their new Kindness Pal. Ask them to be mindful of other people's bodies when they choose their space. Use this as an opportunity to model moving mindfully.

Ask the children to choose the first leader. When you say "Go," the leader starts doing slow movements and the other person tries to follow those movements. Give them a minute or more and then say "Switch" and have them switch roles.

Encourage the children to focus on what their bodies feel like when they are moving.

You might say: *Notice how heavy your arms feel when you hold them out in front of you.*

Ask: When you are finished you can ask the students to share what it felt like to play the game. What was easy and hard about it.

Closing words: *Okay, our time is up for today. Thank you for a great class, everyone. Let's have a nice quiet moment for the bell. If you want to, you can close your eyes, picture your new Kindness Pal, and imagine yourself doing something kind for them this week.*

Ring the bell.

Week 31
Conflict C.A.T. Role Play 1

MINDFULNESS PRACTICE: Body Scan

OBJECTIVES: Practice the Conflict Resolution skills taught in previous lessons.

Practice kindness.

PREPARE: A bell or chime

Copy "Conflict C.A.T. Role Play Scenarios" (in Resource Section) and cut into strips. Alternatively, you may write your own conflicts on slips of paper or index cards.

Have a poster of the Conflict Escalator, the Conflict C.A.T., and the Toolbox up where the kids can see them. See Resource Section.

Your Kindness Pals list

Today students will have another chance to put the Conflict C.A.T. to work in a series of conflict scenarios. If there are conflicts present in your classroom, feel free to add your own scenarios as well. Through Conflict C.A.T. practice, your students are developing a common language and skill set that will allow them to de-escalate conflicts and solve many conflicts on their own. Such important skills!

Mindfulness Practice

Invite today's Mindfulness Helper (MH) to come to the front of the class to sit next to you on a chair (or next to you on the floor).

Say: *Let's all be happy for _____. (sign language applause)*

Prompt the MH to say: "Let's get into our mindful bodies. Let's close our eyes or look down. Let's take three deep breaths."

Say: *Today we are going to take a little trip around our bodies with our minds. You might remember that we did this earlier in the year.*

I want you to start by thinking about the top of your head. Imagine that you can touch the top of your head, not with your hand, but with your mind. It's like you're touching the top of your head from the inside. Can you feel anything when you focus your mind on the top of your head? **Pause**.

Now let's travel down into our faces. Try to feel your forehead—does it feel tight and scrunched? What does it feel like if you try to make it feel more relaxed and smooth? Notice your mouth—is it hanging loose and down? Notice what it feels like if you smile a little bit. **Pause.** *Try to notice your ears—can you feel your ears with your mind? Let's travel down to your neck and shoulders. Notice if your shoulders are tight and high. What does it feel like if you soften and lower your shoulders a bit?* **Pause.**

Let the attention travel down your right arm all the way down to your fingers. Do you remember how your hands felt after you clapped them together? Does your hand feel different now? What do you notice? Let your attention travel down your other arm to your other hand. What do you notice there? Now let your mind travel down your back. Is your back nice and straight or are you hunched over? Notice what it feels like to have a nice, straight back.

Notice the weight of your body on the chair or on the rug or cushion. Let your mind travel down your legs. Do your legs feel the same or different from each other? Try to pay attention to each one of your toes. Give them a little wiggle. Now bring your attention back up to the top of your head and try to sweep down through your whole body. Which foot is warmer?

Now listen for the sound of the bell. When you hear that sound it will be time to open your eyes.

Signal the MH to ring the bell.

Ask the MH to return to their seat.

Conflict Resolution Practice

1. **Review Conflict Escalator, what makes a good apology, and the Conflict Resolution Toolbox**

   Say: *So we've learned a lot about working out conflicts so far. We've learned about how to use our breathing to help us to Calm Down. We've learned about how to apologize well. We've learned eight tools to use to work out conflicts. So let's see if we can put it all together.*

2. Conflict Scenarios

You might say: Today I'm going to ask you to work with your Kindness Pal (or assign a partner).

I am going to give each of you a conflict to work out in a role play. You'll have a few minutes to work out how you are going to do it and to think about which tool you are going to use. There are a few guidelines:

- *Make sure that your role play shows all the parts of the Conflict C.A.T.*
- *You can show us how you go up the Conflict Escalator a little bit (this is fun), but then we want to see how you come down.*
- *One of you has to say "Uh oh, we're going up the Conflict Escalator." You have to show that you are taking some deep breaths. At least one of you has to apologize.*
- *Then you need to show us that you are using one of the tools in the Toolbox.*
- *No bad language and no touching each other.*

Agreed?

When time is up, I'll choose some pairs to come up and show us what you've done.

3. Role Plays

When everyone is paired up, pass out the conflicts and ring a bell. Ring it again when time is up. Be flexible with the time.

The real learning is coming from this part of the process so don't rush it!

After you ring the bell, ask some pairs to come up and show the class what they've come up with.

Make sure that they have covered all of the Conflict C.A.T. steps.

Kindness Pals

Invite students to share what they did for their pals over the last week.

Assign new Kindness Pals after they are finished sharing.

Kindness Pals Activity: Three Questions

Say: *Now that you know who your Kindness Pal is, we're going to find out a little more about them. Who can think of a question that we could ask our Kindness Pal?*

Listen to students' suggestions. They might suggest asking about their favorite color or favorite food or sport.

Choose three questions.

Ask the students to sit with their Kindness Pals and have a little chat.

Share. If you have time, you can come back together as a group and ask them to share something that they learned about their Kindness Pals. This exercise is a great way to practice Mindful Listening and help them to develop an interest in others.

Closing words: *Okay, our time is up for today. Thank you for a great class, everyone. Let's have a nice quiet moment for the bell. If you want to, you can close your eyes, picture your new Kindness Pal, and imagine yourself doing something kind for them this week.*

Ring the bell.

Week 32
Conflict C.A.T. Role Play 2

MINDFULNESS PRACTICE: Cup of Gratitude

OBJECTIVES: Reinforce the Conflict C.A.T. through role playing.

Practice kindness.

PREPARE: A bell or chime

Display posters of the Conflict Escalator, the Conflict C.A.T., and the Toolbox where kids can see them (see Resource Section)

Your Kindness Pals list

As you can tell, we believe that practice, practice, practice is key to successful conflict resolution! Today is our culminating Conflict C.A.T. day. Through a role play they develop themselves, students have a chance to integrate all they have been learning this year.

Mindfulness Practice

Say: Today we're going to repeat a mindfulness practice that we learned back in the Gratitude Unit called *A Cup of Gratitude*.

Invite today's Mindfulness Helper (MH) to come to the front of the class to sit next to you on a chair (or next to you on the floor).

Say: *Let's all be happy for _____.* (sign language applause)

Prompt the MH to say: "Let's get into our mindful bodies. Let's close our eyes or look down. Let's take three deep breaths."

Say: *So let's begin.*

Let's start by making our gratitude cups with our hands.

Now try to think about someone at home that you see every day or almost every day that you are thankful or grateful for. Think of someone who helps you and is kind to you. Now imagine that you can hold them in your little Cup of Gratitude.

Now let's take a deep breath in and as you breathe out, whisper "thank you" into your little cup.

Maybe there is a special animal in your life such as a pet or a stuffed animal or an animal in the wild. Imagine that they are in your little Cup of Gratitude. Let's send some thanks to that animal. Take a deep breath in and as you breathe out, whisper "thank you" into your little cup.

Next, let's think about someone in your class who is kind to you. Imagine that they are in your little Cup of Gratitude. Let's send some thanks to that person. Take a deep breath in and as you breathe out, whisper "thank you" into your little cup.

Take a moment to soak in this feeling of gratitude. Notice what it feels like to be grateful and to say thank you. Remember that you can do this practice on your own anytime.

Let's take a deep breath in and stretch your arms up over your head and then slowly float your arms down as you breathe out. Let's listen for the sound of the bell and we'll open our eyes or look up when we can't hear it anymore.

Say: *In a moment you will hear the sound of the bells and that will mean that it is time to open your eyes or look up. So just get ready for that.*

Ask the MH to ring the bell and return to their seat.

Conflict Resolution Practice

In this lesson, students will create their own conflict and conflict resolution scenarios. Their process should reflect all of the parts of the Conflict C.A.T. and the Conflict Escalator.

This type of practice is essential if the students are to develop the ability to use these tools in real situations.

You might say: *Today we are going to be role-playing again. But this time you are going to work with a partner to create your own conflict.*

1. **Assign partners.**

   You could assign new Kindness Pals or use last week's Kindness Pal pairings.

Say: *Just like last time, your skit needs to show all the parts of the Conflict C.A.T. You can show us how you go up the Conflict Escalator a little bit (this is fun), but then we want to see how you come down. The rules are the same as before:*

- *Make sure that your role play shows all the parts of the Conflict C.A.T.*
- *You can show us how you go up the Conflict Escalator a little bit, but then we want to see how you come down.*
- *One of you has to say, "Uh oh, we're going up the Conflict Escalator." You have to show that you are taking some deep breaths. At least one of you has to apologize.*
- *Then you need to show us that you are using one of the tools in the Toolbox.*
- *No bad language and no touching each other.*

Agreed? When time is up I'll choose some pairs to come up and show us what you've done.

2. **Role Plays**

    Walk around and check in with each pair. Key points to emphasize:

    - Make sure that they are role-playing something appropriate and realistic.
    - Ask them what tool they are planning to use.
    - Encourage them not to spend too much time going up the Conflict Escalator but rather to focus on coming down.

3. **Sharing**

    Ask for volunteers to share their skit with the class. Ask the audience to pay attention to the breathing practices and conflict resolution tools being used as well as whether the apologies pass the "MOFL" test.

Reflect and Discuss

This lesson has given students a chance to put all of their Peace of Mind skills to work. These are skills that not all children or adults have.

Ask how they will put them to work now that they have them? When could their skills be useful at school? at home?

Kindness Pals

Invite students to share what they did for their pals over the last week.

Assign new Kindness Pals if you haven't already. These will be our last Kindness Pal pairs for the year!

If you have time, choose one of the Kindness Pal Activities your class has particularly enjoyed for the new Pals to do together.

Closing words: *Okay, our time is up for today. Thank you for a great class, everyone. Let's have a nice quiet moment for the bell. If you want to, you can close your eyes, picture your new Kindness Pal, and imagine yourself doing something kind for them this week.*

Ring the bell.

Year-End Activity

Week 33
Kindest Things

MINDFULNESS PRACTICE: Heartfulness

OBJECTIVES: Encourage the children to see the good in each other and experience the good feeling of sharing heartfelt compliments.

PREPARE: Paper, pen, or pencil for every student in the class

Here we are, the last Peace of Mind Class for the year! Congratulations on taking your students through a year of learning and self-discovery. We hope you enjoy this final lesson!

> NOTE FROM LINDA: *This is a wonderful activity that has been very meaningful to my students over the years. It is a bit time-consuming for the teacher because you are going to be typing up a page for each child that lists all of the kind things the class said about him or her. I hope that you will do it anyway.*
>
> *I have found that I learn more about my students from what they say about other people than from what others say about them. I have had many students tell me that they have kept their Kindest Things page on their walls all the way through college! It's worth the work. I've done it for up to 100 kids every year and it is time well-spent.*

Mindfulness Practice

Invite today's Mindfulness Helper (MH) to come to the front of the class to sit next to you on a chair.

Say: *Let's all be happy for _____.* (sign language applause)

Prompt the MH to say: "Let's get into our mindful bodies. Let's close our eyes or look down. Let's take three deep breaths."

Say: *Today we're going to practice Heartfulness. Let's start by thinking about someone who makes you happy. Choose someone you see every day at home or at school. You might choose someone in your family, a friend, a teacher, even a pet. Just choose someone and try to picture that person happy and smiling. Picture them doing something that makes them happy. Try to notice how you feel when you think about this person.*

Now, if you'd like to, fill your heart up with kindness and repeat these words in your mind while you think about this person:

May you be happy. **Wait a moment.**

May you be healthy. **Wait a moment.**

May you be peaceful. **Wait a moment.**

Take a moment to notice how you feel. Any way that you feel is fine, even if you feel nothing. Just try to notice it.

Invite the students to share whom they were thinking about.

Now take a deep breath, and listen for the sound of the bell. When you hear that sound it will be time to open your eyes.

Ask the MH to ring the bell and return to their seat.

Kindness Practice

These instructions are long. It's really important that the kids get the sense of reverence in this activity.

1. **Set the Tone**

Say: *Today we are going to do something very powerful. We have talked about how we can use our words to hurt or to help others. Today we are going to use our words to be kind to each other.*

I am going to ask you to think about the kindest thing you can think of to say about each person in the class.

We are going to go one by one. I will say the name of someone in the class and write that person's name on the board. You will write down one or two things about that person.

*Think about what is special about that person—a talent they have, a time when they were kind to you, maybe they are always friendly to new people, maybe they always make you laugh, maybe you admire them for being brave, or creative or artistic, etc. Do **not** just use the first thing that pops into your head.*

You will write your name on your paper, but only I will see it. Each comment will be anonymous.

IMPORTANT: There will be absolutely no talking during this exercise. We are holding each person in the class in our kindness circle. Giggling or talking can sometimes lead to accidental unkindness or misunderstandings. Anyone who cannot abide by the rule of silence will be asked to wait in the hall and will not participate.

After class I will type up a paper for each one of you with all of the kindness things your classmates said about you. You won't be able to see who said what, but you will see what they said. This will take me a while, but I will return them to you soon. Make sure that you share your paper with your family!

2. **Lead the Class through the Exercise**

   Write the first student's name on the board so everyone can see the spelling.

   Say: *"Now we will think about (Name). What is the kindest thing you can think of to say about (Name)? What is special about (Name)?"*

   Give a minute or more for each child depending on how much time you have.

   Give them time to catch up on anybody they missed and then collect the papers.

3. **Ask the class to share what this experience was like for them.**

   You might ask: *How did writing kind things about your classmates make you feel?*

4. **Putting it all together for your students**

It's up to you now to create a list of kind things for each of your students. Of course you won't say who said what; simply list the positive statements. We hope you have time to enjoy this process and appreciate the connections you've made in your classroom.

Kindness Pals

Invite Kindness Pals to share the kind things they did for each other during the last week. Do not give out new Pals.

Closing words: *This is our last class together, so I will not be handing out new Kindness Pals today.*

I hope that you enjoyed learning more about mindfulness and kindness and how to work out our conflicts peacefully. The world needs lots of kind, mindful people. Now you have some tools to help you go out into the world and make it a more peaceful place. I hope you will.

Resources

Program Extensions

Consider moving the lessons of Peace of Mind beyond the classroom with one or more of these Program extensions. Each offers opportunities for students to hone their new mindfulness skills, to practice kindness, and to use the common language and tools they are learning to resolve conflicts.

Daily Mindful Moments

The *Peace of Mind Curriculum* is designed to be used in a weekly class. If you have the time and desire to make Peace of Mind a part of your classroom every day, wonderful! Daily Mindful Moments are a great way for your students to practice the skills that they are learning weekly in Peace of Mind class and to enjoy a moment of calm and quiet before beginning a new activity. It just takes a couple of minutes. Once you get into the habit, it will be something that is beneficial to both you and your students.

You may want to make "Mindfulness Helper" a weekly job in your classroom and have that student lead the Daily Mindful Moment. You may decide to lead the Daily Mindful Moment yourself at the beginning to set the tone and expectations and then transition to a student-led practice. Either way is fine. You can also experiment with the duration of the quiet moment. Some classes will have no problem with two minutes and will quickly graduate to more; some classes will be better off with one minute or less to start.

Peace Club

Peace Club is a lunch and recess program for students who need a smaller alternative to the cafeteria and the playground. It can be a mixed-age group of anywhere from 20-50 students. Peace Club is meant to be a comfortable option for kids who sometimes struggle with their social skills or with being in a large group. It is also popular among kids who like to make a difference and who make a commitment to making everyone feel welcome and respected.

At Lafayette Elementary School, for example, children on the autism spectrum and with other diagnoses often have Peace Club specifically written into their IEP's and 504 plans because Peace Club provides some structured play as well as informal group counseling during the hour. Peace Club requires all students who come to make a promise to treat everyone else with kindness and respect and to make sure that conflicts are worked out peacefully and everyone is included. Fourth and fifth

graders might serve as special helpers. These are kids who make an extra commitment to seek out those who have a harder time jumping in and include them in games, and who help others work out conflicts peacefully.

Peace Heroes

Peace Heroes is a way to recognize children who make an extra effort to be kind. One way to do this is to have a box somewhere in the school where kids or adults can write a note recognizing another student for an act of kindness. The names can be posted on a bulletin board somewhere in the school. Once a month some of the names can be read on school-wide announcements.

Linkages to Behavior Management Programs

The concepts underlying the Peace of Mind Program can be adapted to work with classroom management programs like Positive Behavioral Intervention and Supports (PBIS) or Responsive Classroom. School-wide expectations can be expressed in "mindful" language—for example, "Speak Mindfully, Act Mindfully, Move Mindfully." Most of the things that we are expecting the children to do at school fall into these three categories. Children can be encouraged to "move mindfully" in the hallways, instead of saying "no running!"; or to "speak mindfully" instead of "don't blurt out," or to "act mindfully" instead of "be responsible." This subtle shift in language can help children understand the reasons for our rules and make them more likely to follow them.

Applications to Social Justice

In the Summer of 2020, Peace of Mind published its 17-lesson Social Justice Lesson Supplement to help educators engage in challenging, important conversations with 3rd through 5th grade students related to our national reckoning with race and racism. This set of lessons teaches mindfulness not only as a means to help students manage big emotions, but also as a skill to help them become kind and courageous peacemakers and agents of positive change. These lessons are designed to be taught in conjunction with the *Peace of Mind Core Curriculum for Third Grade* and/or the *Peace of Mind Curriculum for Fourth and Fifth Grades*. This lesson supplement is available as a free download here: TeachPeaceofMind.org/shop/.

Reproducible Materials

All of the worksheets and skits included in this curriculum are original works by Linda Ryden, written specifically for the *Peace of Mind Curriculum*.

In this section you will find the materials referred to in the "Prepare" section of each lesson. Feel free to make copies for your students.

Week	Worksheets & Skits Needed
All Weeks	Kindness Pals list
Week 1	My Kindness Pals Worksheet
Week 4	Create Your Own Breath Worksheet
Week 8	Little Good Things Worksheet
Week 9	My Kindness Pals Favorite Things Worksheet
Week 19	Heartfulness Worksheet
Week 20	"Should We Let Him Play?" Skit
Unit 6	Diagram of the Brain for Classroom
Week 24	"Rosie's Brain" Skit
Unit 7	Conflict Escalator, C.A.T., Conflict Toolbox Posters
Week 26	"Scrabble vs. Monopoly" Skits
Weeks 27, 30	"The Class Party 1" and "The Class Party 2" Skits
Week 31	Conflict C.A.T. Role Play Scenarios

Kindness Pals

for the week of _____

           Student   Student

1.

2.

3.

4.

5.

6.

7.

8.

9.

10.

11.

12.

13.

14.

15.

Week 1
My Kindness Pal Worksheet

Here are some kind acts I can do for my pal. Circle all those you might choose.

Get backpack   Eat lunch together   Small gift   Compliment

Draw a picture   Stack chair   Play at recess   Another idea

Week 4
Create Your Own Breath

My Breath is called: _____

Breathe slowly in and out.

Your Name: _____

Week 8
Ten Little Good Things

Your Name: _____

1. _____

2. _____

3. _____

4. _____

5. _____

6. _____

7. _____

8. _____

9. _____

10. _____

Week 9
My Kindness Pal's Favorite Things Interview Worksheet

Your name _____

Your Pal's Name_____

Note:
Extra points for finding out the "why" as in "Why is that your favorite animal?"

1. Favorite furry animal
2. Favorite feathery animal
3. Favorite lunch
4. Least favorite lunch
5. Favorite vegetable
6. Least favorite vegetable
7. Favorite time of day
8. Favorite kind of weather
9. Least favorite kind of weather
10. Favorite thing to wear
11. Least favorite thing to wear
12. Favorite kind of pasta
13. Favorite pizza topping
14. Favorite thing about your family
15. Favorite family tradition

Bonus questions:
Peanut butter - crunchy or creamy or not at all?
Sushi or tacos?
Minecraft or Fortnite or huh?
Basketball or soccer?
Can you roll your tongue?
Name an everyday food that you have never tasted

Week 19

Heartfulness Worksheet

I sent my kind thoughts to...

May you be happy.
May you be healthy and strong.
May you be peaceful.

Week 20
Should We Let Him Play? Skit

By Linda Ryden

Topic: Kindness, Inclusion

Characters: Jason, Susan, Beth, Jerry, Mark

Setting: Recess on playground

4 friends are playing together and 1 new kid is sitting alone

Jason: Boy, I'm so glad it stopped raining! I hate indoor recess.

Susan: Me too! It's so hot in the school today.

Beth: What do you want to do? Play basketball?

Jason: Sure.

Jerry: (*looking over at Mark*) Hey, have you guys noticed that the new kid is always alone at recess?

Jason: Who cares? He's not our friend.

Susan: Yeah, we've got enough friends. He should make his own friends.

Beth: I heard that he's weird. I heard that he never talks to anyone.

Jerry: Well, he looks pretty sad and lonely. I remember when I was new at school. It was pretty scary. Nobody talked to me for a whole week.

Jason: Well, if you care so much about him, why don't you go over and play with him?

Susan: Yeah, just don't bring him over here! I don't want to play with that new kid.

Beth: Me neither. Let's go play.

Jerry: Come on, you guys! You know that it's mean to leave people out. Sometimes when people get left out all of the time they might get bullied.

Jason: You're right. When my brother was little he was always by himself because the other kids wouldn't play with him. Then a big kid started picking on him.

Beth: Gee, that's awful.

Susan: Maybe we should go over and ask him if he wants to play with us.

Beth: But he's just going to say no.

Jason: Yeah, he doesn't want to talk to anyone. He probably wants to be alone.

Susan: I don't think anyone really wants to be alone. Let's go over and try.

All: Okay.

Jason: Hi. I'm Jason. Do you want to play basketball with us?

Mark: Um, no thanks.

Jerry: Come on, it will be fun! Do you know how to play basketball?

Mark: Sure! At my old school I was on the basketball team. We won a championship.

Beth: Wow! I want you on my team!

Jason: No, be on my team!

Susan: We'll just flip a coin, okay?

Mark: Okay. Thanks!

Jerry: Come on you guys, let's go play.

All walk off happily.

Unit 6
Diagram of Three Parts of the Brain

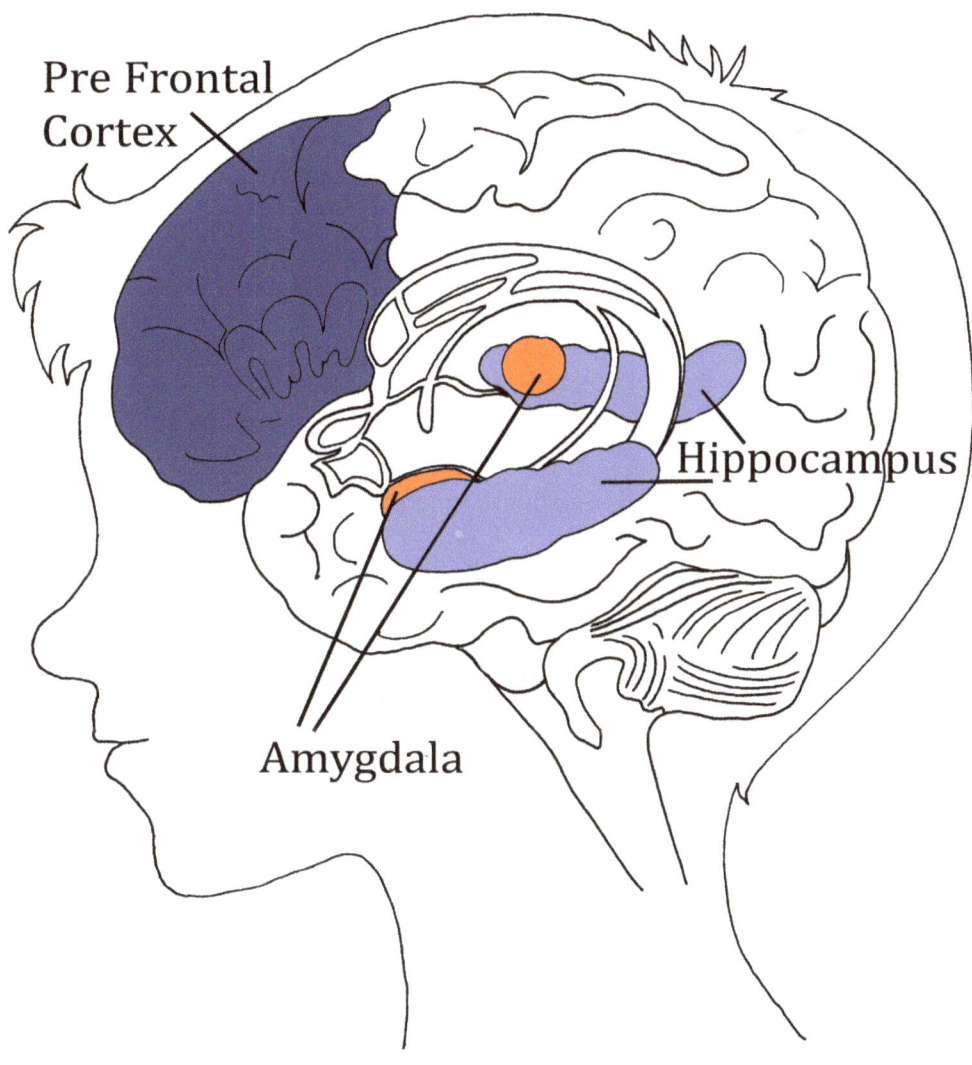

Week 24
Rosie's Brain Skit

By Linda Ryden

Topic: Understanding our brains

Characters: Rosie's Mom, Rosie, Henry, Amygdala, Hippocampus, Prefrontal Cortex (PFC)

Setting: Rosie's home and school

Rosie's Mom: Rosie, remember, you have a piano lesson after school today.

Rosie: Okay!

Rosie's Mom: Don't forget!

Later that day at school:

Henry: Hey Rosie, do you want to come over after school today?

Rosie: Hmmm… (*looks like she's thinking and reacting to what her brain is saying*)

Amygdala: Oh my gosh! That's so exciting! I love playing with Henry! Yay yay yay!!!!!!!!!!!!!!!!!!

Hippocampus: Oh Rosie…. Don't you remember that you have a piano lesson after school today?

Amygdala: Oh nooooo! That's the worst news ever!!! I'm devastated. I'm going to freak out and scream!!!

PFC: Hang on now, Amygdala. Are you sure that's the best idea? Maybe we can come up with a solution to this problem.

Amygdala: No, there is no solution! It's a disaster, it's the worst thing that has ever happened (*breathing hard*).

PFC: Now, now, don't flip your lid. Why don't you do your mindful breathing?

Hippocampus: Oh I remember that! We learned about it in Peace Class. It's

when you breathe in and out to help you to calm down.

PFC: That's right. Let's give it a try.

Rosie and Amygdala start taking deep breaths.

Amygdala: Hey, I'm starting to feel better.

Rosie: Me too! Maybe this isn't the worst problem ever.

Hippocampus: You know, I remember other times when throwing tantrums didn't turn out very well and made things worse.

PFC: Me too. Now that you've calmed down, Amygdala, I think I have come up with a solution to the problem. Why don't we get together with Henry after your piano lesson?

Amygdala: That's a great idea! Thanks, PFC!

Hippocampus: Remember the last time you had a playdate with Henry and you ate pizza together?

Amygdala: That's right! Maybe we can do that again today.

PFC: Why don't we ask him?

Rosie: Hey Henry, I have a piano lesson after school so can we have our playdate afterwards and maybe eat some pizza?

Henry: Sounds great!!

All: Yay!!

Unit 7
Conflict Resolution

The Conflict Escalator

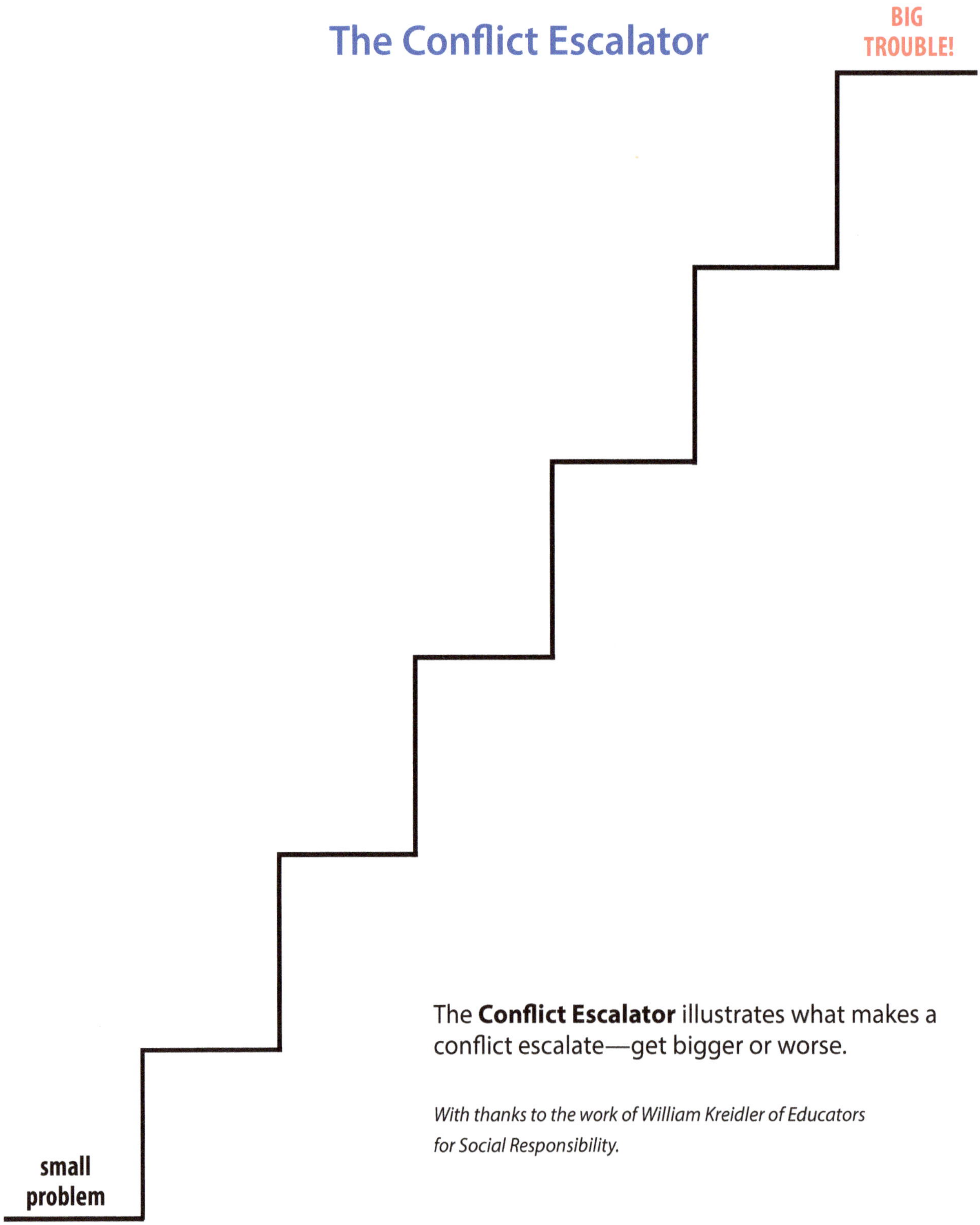

BIG TROUBLE!

small problem

The **Conflict Escalator** illustrates what makes a conflict escalate—get bigger or worse.

With thanks to the work of William Kreidler of Educators for Social Responsibility.

Unit 7
Conflict Resolution

The Conflict C.A.T.

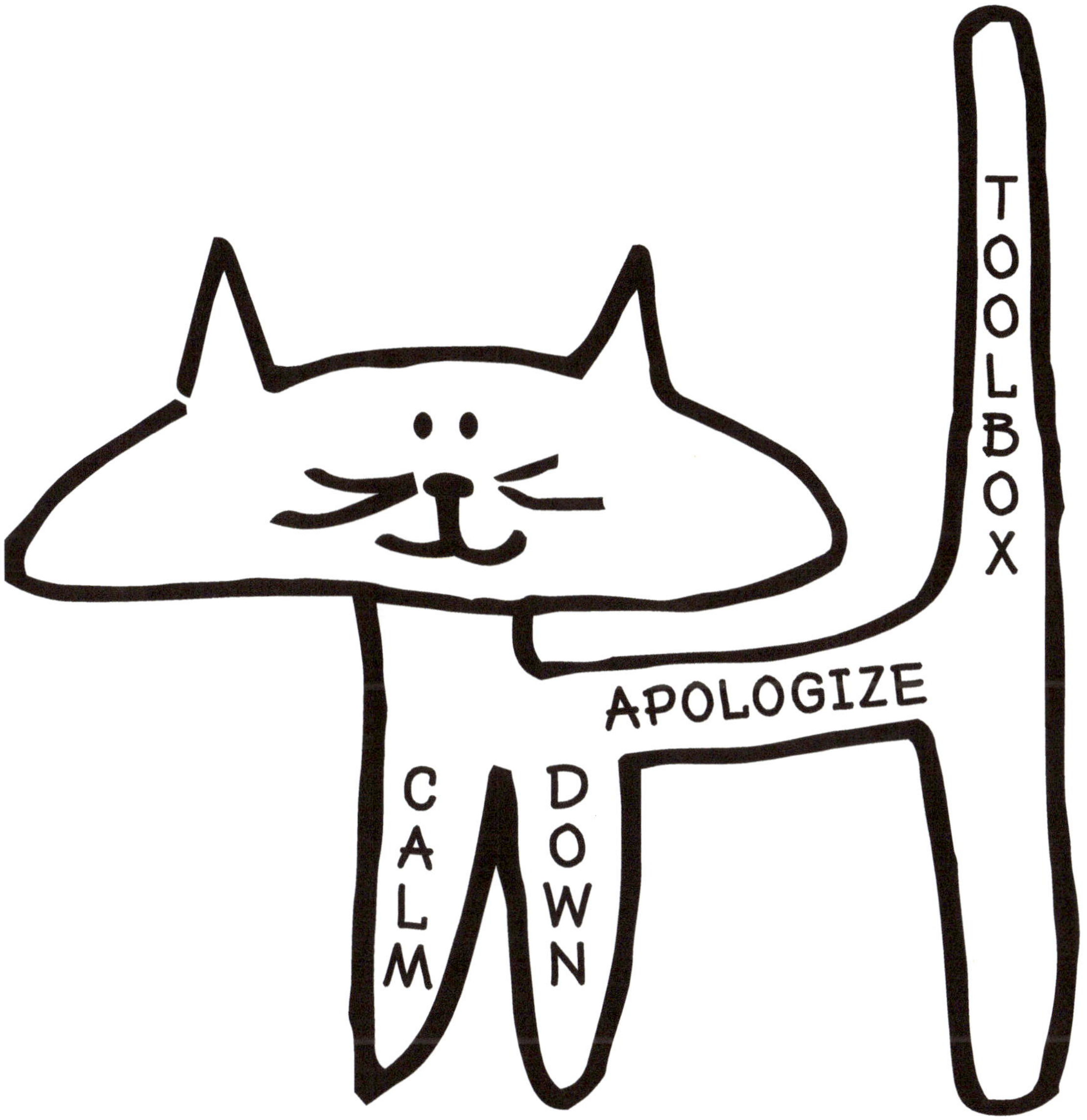

Unit 7
Conflict Resolution

The Conflict Toolbox

1. Share
2. Take Turns
3. Be Kind
4. Leave it to Chance
5. Compromise
6. Pause the Conflict
7. Skip the Conflict
8. Get Help

Week 26
Scrabble vs. Monopoly 1 Skit

By Linda Ryden

Topic: Conflict Resolution
Characters: Charlie, Henry, Julio, Lucy, Reign, Alice
Scene: Charlie's house. The kids are having a playdate.

Charlie: Hey guys, let's play Monopoly! I just got a new game and I've been really wanting to play it.

Henry: That sounds great! I love Monopoly!

Julio: Yes! Monopoly is my favorite game!

Lucy: No way! Monopoly takes too long to play. Let's play Scrabble instead!

Reign: Yeah, Scrabble is awesome. I'm really good!

Alice: That's because you're a really good speller.

Reign: Thanks!

Charlie: What are you guys talking about? Monopoly is the coolest game. Scrabble is for geeks.

Lucy: Who are you calling a geek? You're a loser.

Henry: Yeah, Scrabble is boring. Only boring people like to play Scrabble.

Reign: If you guys are going to play Monopoly then Lucy and Alice and I are leaving!

Charlie: Fine with me! We don't like playing with dumb girls anyway!

Lucy, **Reign**, and **Alice** storm out.

Week 26 and 30
Scrabble vs. Monopoly 2 Skit

By Linda Ryden

Topic: Conflict Resolution
Characters: Charlie, Henry, Julio, Lucy, Reign, Alice
Scene: Charlie's house. The kids are having a playdate.

Charlie: Hey guys, let's play Monopoly! I just got a new game and I've been really wanting to play it.

Henry: That sounds great! I love Monopoly!

Julio: Yes! Monopoly is my favorite game!

Lucy: No way! Monopoly takes too long to play. Let's play Scrabble instead!

Reign: Yeah, Scrabble is awesome. I'm really good!

Alice: That's because you're a really good speller.

Reign: Thanks!

Charlie: What are you talking about? Monopoly is the coolest game. Scrabble is for geeks!

Lucy: Who are you calling a geek? You're a loser.

Henry: Hey you guys, we're going up the Conflict Escalator.

Reign: Oh, you're right. There's nothing but trouble at the top of the Conflict Escalator!

Julio: Why don't we calm down a bit? Let's take some deep breaths.

Everybody stops and takes three deep breaths.

Lucy: Hey, Charlie, I'm sorry I called you a loser. I didn't mean it.

Charlie: No, I'm sorry. I shouldn't have said Scrabble is for geeks. I like Scrabble. I was just really excited to play Monopoly and I got carried away.

Alice: I have an idea! Why don't we take turns. We can play Monopoly today and then tomorrow we can go over to my house and play Scrabble.

All: That's a great idea!

Week 27
The Class Party 1 Skit

By Linda Ryden

Topic: Conflict Resolution
Characters: Richard Leslie, Carlos, Diana, Oscar
Scene: Classroom during indoor recess.

Richard: I'm so excited about this party!

Oscar: Yeah, me too. I can't believe the teacher is letting us come up with the theme.

Frankie: I know, it's going to be awesome! I think we should have a chocolate theme. We could fill the entire classroom with chocolate and just swim around in it for the whole day!

All: Frankie!

Diana: Frankie, that is a ridiculous idea. Although it does sound like fun. We have to come up with something the teacher will actually let us do.

Richard: How about a craft party? We could set up lots of stations and make a bunch of different crafts.

Lesie: Nah, that sounds boring. I think we should have a Star Wars theme.

Oscar: Yeah, we could have huge light saber fights!

Frankie: Cool! And the light sabers could be made of chocolate.

All: Frankie!

Diana: Not everybody likes Star Wars and the fighting sounds too violent. I like the craft idea.

Leslie: No, Star Wars!

Oscar: Yeah — I want to dress up like Darth Vader!

Diana: Star Wars is stupid! I agree with Richard — a craft party is something everybody would like.

Leslie: Star Wars isn't stupid, you're stupid!

Richard: Ouch! That's cold!

Oscar: Seriously. This is getting out of hand.

Diana: Well, fine. Maybe the teacher will let us have separate parties.

Leslie: That would be great—that way we don't have to talk to you anymore.

Diana: Fine with me!

Everyone storms out.

Week 27
The Class Party 2 Skit

By Linda Ryden

Topic: Conflict Resolution
Characters: Richard, Leslie, Carlos, Diana, Oscar
Scene: Classroom during indoor recess

Richard: I'm so excited about this party!

Oscar: Yeah, me too. I can't believe the teacher is letting us come up with the theme.

Frankie: I know, it's going to be awesome! I think we should have a chocolate theme. We could fill the entire classroom with chocolate and just swim around in it for the whole day!

All: Frankie!

Diana: Frankie, that is a ridiculous idea. Although it does sound like fun. We have to come up with something the teacher will actually let us do.

Richard: How about a craft party? We could set up lots of stations and make a bunch of different crafts.

Lesie: Nah, that sounds boring. I think we should have a Star Wars theme.

Oscar: Yeah, we could have huge light saber fights!

Frankie: Cool! And the light sabers could be made of chocolate.

All: Frankie!

Diana: Not everybody likes Star Wars and the fighting sounds too violent. I like the craft idea.

Leslie: No, Star Wars!

Oscar: Yeah — I want to dress up like Darth Vader!

Diana: Star Wars is stupid! I agree with Richard — a craft party is something everybody would like.

Leslie: Star Wars isn't stupid, you're stupid!

Richard: Ouch! That's cold!

Oscar: Seriously. This is getting out of hand.

Diana: Hang on, we're going up the Conflict Escalator! If we keep fighting, we're never going to come up with an idea, and we might not get to have the party.

Richard: She's right. We need to calm down. Let's take some deep breaths.

Everybody takes three slow deep breaths.

Leslie: I'm sorry I said you are stupid, Diana. I really didn't mean it. I was just flipping my lid.

Diana: I'm sorry too. Star Wars isn't stupid.

Frankie: How about having a "Go Green" party? We all care about the environment. We could make posters to put up around the school reminding people to recycle and stuff.

Diana: And we could make bird feeders out of pine cones and peanut butter and birdseed.

Richard: Cool! And we could even make light sabers out of recycled paper towel rolls.

Frankie: And we could have a dunk tank filled with chocolate!

All: Frankie!!!

Everybody high fives each other.

Week 31
Conflict C.A.T. Role Play Scenarios

Copy and cut apart to hand to your students.

Two kids are arguing about what to name the class hamster.

Two kids are arguing over who gets to go first in Checkers.

Two kids can't agree on what kind of pizza to have.

Two kids argue over whether to play four square or go on the monkey bars during recess.

Two kids argue over what kind of animal is the most dangerous.

Two kids argue about whether gummy bears or Skittles are better.

Two kids argue over whose turn it is to choose the movie.

Two kids argue about who gets to use the family computer.

Two kids argue about whether any words rhyme with orange.

Two kids argue over whether Superman or Captain Marvel is stronger.

Two kids argue over what is the best ice cream flavor.

Resources to Support You and Your Teaching

Here are just a few of the many books, apps, podcasts, and websites we've found helpful. Each of them will point you to other resources. Enjoy!

Your Own Mindfulness Practice

Apps

Headspace.com
Ten Percent Happier App and Podcast
Calm, especially Jeff Warren's Daily Trip and How To Meditate Series

Online Mindfulness Courses

Mindful Schools Courses for Educators
https://www.mindfulschools.org/

Elements of Meditation with Jeff Warren
https://jeffwarren.THiNKific.com/courses/

Good Reads

You Belong: A Call for Connection by Sebene Selassie

The Mindful Athlete by George Mumford

Ten Percent Happier and Meditation for Fidgety Skeptics by Dan Harris and Jeff Warren

Hardwiring Happiness by Dr. Rick Hanson

Teaching Mindfulness

Mindfulness for Teachers: Simple skills for peace and productivity in the classroom by Patricia Jennings

The Way of Mindful Education: Cultivating Well-being in Teachers and Students by Daniel Rechtschaffen & Jon Kabat-Zinn PhD

Compassion and Gratitude

Real Love by Sharon Salzberg

Center for the Greater Good at U.C. Berkeley
https://greatergood.berkeley.edu/

Center for Healthy Minds at the U. of Wisconsin
https://centerhealthyminds.org/

Brain Science

Daniel Siegel's Brain Talk Video (YouTube)
http://www.drdansiegel.com/resources/everyday_mindsight_tools/

Trauma Sensitive Teaching

Jennings, P. A. (2019). *The Trauma-Sensitive Classroom: Building Resilience with Compassionate Teaching*. New York: W.W. Norton & Company.

Treleaven, David (2018). *Trauma-Sensitive Mindfulness: Practices for Safe and Transformative Healing*. New York: W. W. Norton & Company.

Teaching for Social Justice

Starting in Grade 4, lessons in our *Peace of Mind Core Curriculum Series* include the application of Mindfulness-based SEL to social justice topics like identity, discrmination, bias and standing up to injustice. Though your students won't receive these lessons for another year, you might like to learn more about some of these topics now as a way to support your teaching in general.

Here are some options:

Why We Can't Afford Whitewashed Social and Emotional Learning by
Dr. Dena Simmons
http://www.ascd.org/publications/newsletters/education_update/apr19/vol61/num04/Why_We_Can't_Afford_Whitewashed_Social-Emotional_Learning.aspx

Racial Healing Allies
https://www.ticiess.com/racial-healing-allies

AntiRacist Table
theantiracisttable.com

LiberatED
denasimmons.com

Learning for Justice
learningforjustice.org

Center for AntiRacist Education
antiracistfuture.org

Bibliography

Bradshaw, C. P. (2015). "Translating research to practice in bullying prevention." *American Psychologist*, 70 (4), 322-332.

Breeding, K., & Harrison, J. (2007). *Connected and Respected: Lessons from the Resolving Conflict Creatively Program*. Cambridge, Mass.: Educators for Social Responsibility.

Durlak, J. A., Weissberg, R. P., Dymnicki, A. B., Taylor, R. D. & Schellinger, K. B. (2011). "The impact of enhancing students' social and emotional learning: A meta-analysis of school-based universal interventions." *Child Development*, 82(1), 405–432.

Hanson, R. (2015). *Hardwiring Happiness*. Random House USA.

Jennings, P. (2015). *Mindfulness for Teachers: Simple skills for peace and productivity in the classroom*. The Norton Series on the Social Neuroscience of Education.

Jennings, P. A. (2019). *The Trauma-Sensitive Classroom: Building Resilience with Compassionate Teaching*. New York: W.W. Norton & Company.

Lantieri, Linda. "How SEL and Mindfulness Can Work Together." Greater Good. April 7, 2015. Accessed September 28, 2015. http://greatergood.berkeley.edu/article/item/how_social_emotional_learning_and_mindfulness_can_work_together.

Learning Heroes, *Developing Life Skills in Children: A Road Map for Communicating with Parents*, https://bealearninghero.org/parent-mindsets/ September 2018.

O'Brennan, L., & Bradshaw, C. (2013). "School Climate: A Research Brief". A report prepared for the National Education Association, Washington, D.C.

Rechtschaffen, D., & Kabat-Zinn PhD, J. (2014). *The Way of Mindful Education: Cultivating Well-being in Teachers and Students*. Norton Books in Education.

Schonert-Reichl, K. A., & Lawlor, M. S. (2010). "The effects of a mindfulness-based education program on pre-and early adolescents' well-being and social and emotional competence." *Mindfulness*, 1(3), 137-151.

Schonert-Reichl, K. A., Oberle, E., Lawlor, M. S., Abbott, D., Thomson, K., Oberlander, T. F., & Diamond, A. (2015). "Enhancing cognitive and social–

emotional development through a simple-to-administer mindfulness-based school program for elementary school children: A randomized controlled trial." *Developmental Psychology,* 51(1), 52-66.

Seppala, E., Simon-Thomas, E., Brown, S. L., Worline, M. C., Cameron, C. D., & Doty, J. R. (2017). *The Oxford Handbook of Compassion Science*. New York, NY: Oxford University Press.

Siegel, D. J., & Bryson, T. P. (2012). *The Whole-Brain Child*. London: Constable & Robinson.

Simmons, Dena (2019), *Why We Can't Afford Whitewashed Social-Emotional Learning* Retrieved from http://www.ascd.org/publications/newsletters/education_update/apr19/vol61/num04

Srinivasan, M. (2014). *Teach, Breathe, Learn: Mindfulness in and out of the Classroom*. Berkeley, CA: Parallax Press.

Treleaven, David (2018). *Trauma-Sensitive Mindfulness: Practices for Safe and Transformative Healing*. New York: W. W. Norton & Company.

Weare, K. (2013). "Developing mindfulness with children and young people: A review of the evidence and policy context." *Journal of Children's Services,* 8(2), 141-153.

Zoogman, S., Goldberg, S.B., Hoyt, W.T., & Miller, L. (2015). "Mindfulness interventions with youth: A meta-analysis." *Mindfulness,* 6, 290 - 302.

Zenner, C., Hermleben-Kurz, S., & Walach, H. (2014). "Mindfulness-based interventions in schools: A systematic review and meta-analysis." *Frontiers in Psychology,* 5, article 603.

Credits

Hand Model of the Brain. Lessons 21-24: "Everyday Mindsight Tools." Dr. Dan Siegel. March 17, 2011. Accessed September 28, 2015. http://www.drdansiegel.com/resources/everyday_mindsight_tools/

The Conflict Escalator. Lessons 26-32: Kreidler, William J. *Teaching Conflict Resolution through Children's Literature*. New York: Scholastic Professional Books, 1994

Blooming Breaths. Lessons 13, 18, 29. Peace of Mind Student Alexis Larson, 2021

Appreciation

Linda's students have been our greatest teachers, our inspiration, and our joy. Each one of the thousands of children Linda has worked with at Lafayette Elementary School in Washington, D.C., has taught us something important, and some have left lasting imprints on our hearts. These children, some of who are in college now, fill us with hope that they will create a more peaceful world than the one they were born into.

We owe a huge debt of gratitude to the wonderful teachers at Lafayette Elementary and all of the other Washington DC area schools who have welcomed and supported the Peace of Mind Program from its earliest days. Leaders Liz Whisnant, Megan Vroman, and Jordan Love, especially, have gone above and beyond.

Lafayette's amazing School Counselor, Jillian Diesner, took on the challenge of adapting the *Peace of Mind Curriculum* to our youngest students and has contributed so much of her expertise and creativity to expand Peace of Mind in wonderful new ways.

In this testing-focused culture it takes courage to set aside time in the school day for something that can't be easily quantified. Many thanks to Lafayette Principal Dr. Carrie Broquard for her enthusiastic support for the Peace of Mind Program. Thanks to her leadership and willingness to go out on a limb, Peace of Mind has grown into an effective model program.

Peace of Mind would not have been possible without the generous financial support of the Lafayette Home and School Association. Many thanks to all members, past and present, for supporting the program over the years, and for making our children's social emotional development a priority.

We are grateful to the many people whose work inspires and informs the Peace of Mind Program. So much of what is offered in these pages is inspired by the work of these wonderful teachers: Jeff Warren, Dan Harris, Rick Hanson, Sharon Salzberg, Oren Jay Sofer, Jay Michelson, and Sebene Selassie.

Our nonprofit organization, Peace of Mind Inc, is guided and sustained by an extraordinary Board of Directors. Enormous thanks to Liz Whisnant, Darrel Jodrey, Chapin Springer, Dr. Elizabeth Hoffman, and Subrat Biswal for all that you give and have given. Thanks, too, to our Advisors whose input has been invaluable: Rie Odsbjerg, Jelene Popovic, Jackie Snowden, Avideh Shashaani, Harriet Sanford, Dave Trachtenberg, and Janine Rudder. And finally, a shout-out to volunteer Jenny Sour, whose skillful and insightful editorial help was instrumental in getting this curriculum over the finish line.

Finally, we are deeply grateful to the funders who make our work possible, including The Morris and Gwendolyn Cafritz Foundation, The Bender Foundation, The SuPau Foundation, and The Fund for the Future of Our Children, as well as our wonderful corporate and individual donors. We couldn't do it without you!

With love and gratitude,

Linda   Cheryl

Linda Ryden and Cheryl Cole Dodwell, August 2021

Authors

Linda Ryden is the creator of the Peace of Mind Program and author of the *Peace of Mind Curriculum Series*, a cutting-edge combination of mindfulness-based social-emotional learning, conflict resolution, and social justice for Early Childhood through Middle School. Linda has served as the full-time Peace Teacher at Lafayette Elementary School, Washington D.C.'s largest public elementary schools, since 2003 and continues to teach Peace of Mind classes to more than 700 students every week. Linda is also actively engaged in supporting her school's efforts to sustain an inclusive and equitable school climate.

Linda is the author of five mindfulness-based children's books, including three published by Tilbury House. Her work has been featured in *The Washington Post, Washingtonian Magazine, Washington Parent, Washington Family, Teaching Tolerance,* and *Edutopia,* among others. Linda was a keynote speaker at the National Network of State Teachers of the Year conference in 2020 and a featured speaker at the National Education Association Foundation Symposium in 2018, and has received a Commendation for Educational Innovation from the D.C. Board of Education.

Linda brings a passion for teaching peace and over 25 years of teaching experience to her work with children and adults. Linda lives in Washington, D.C., with her husband Jeremiah Cohen, owner of Bullfrog Bagels, their two children, and their dog Phoebe.

Cheryl Cole Dodwell, the Executive Director of Peace of Mind Inc., is the co-author of the *Peace of Mind Core Curriculum Series* and manages the development of the *Henry and Friends Storybook Series* and all other Peace of Mind resources. Cheryl brings dedication and passion, a love of writing and editing, a background in finance and publishing, education and practice in the management of community organizations, and deep experience in mindfulness, healing practices, and parenting to her work with Peace of Mind. She is grateful to be able to contribute to making our world a kinder and inclusive place for all. Cheryl lives in Maryland with her husband James and loves visits from her two kind and inspiring grown-up children.

Illustrator

Gigi Gonyea is a textile designer and illustrator. She uses color, pattern, and perspective in her designs to create whimsical and joyous spaces. She has a BFA from The Savannah College of Art and Design and is a former Peace of Mind student of Linda Ryden.

www.ingramcontent.com/pod-product-compliance
Lightning Source LLC
Chambersburg PA
CBHW051255110526

44589CB00025B/2841